I0434884

United States
Department of
Agriculture

Forest Service

Gen. Tech. Report
WO-84

April 2010

Meeting Current and Future Conservation Challenges Through the Synthesis of Long-Term Silviculture and Range Management Research

Disclaimer

Contents

Meeting Current and Future Conservation Challenges Through the Synthesis of Long-Term Silviculture and Range Management Research

Executive Summary

The Experimental Forests and Ranges (EFRs) of the Forest Service, U.S. Department of Agriculture were established to represent major forest vegetation types of the United States, to provide guidelines for management of those forests and ranges, and to serve as "outdoor classrooms" for land managers to learn how to better manage their forests. Research data collected during the 100 years since the first experimental forest was established in 1908 can be used synthetically to address regional and continental scale questions related to forest and range management, key forest ecosystem processes, wildlife habitat requirements, watershed management, and other topics.

Toward that end, a workshop was held to advance our knowledge and ability to meet current and future conservation challenges by synthesizing silviculture and range management information from our network of EFRs. Sixty scientists from Forest Service Research and Development and partner institutions participated in the workshop, which was held at the U.S. Fish & Wildlife Service National Conservation Training Center in Shepherdstown, WV, from September 29 to October 2, 2008.

To lay the groundwork, researchers who have worked with EFR data, or who have been involved in similar synthesis activities, described their experiences. Short courses provided an introduction to novel statistical techniques particularly useful for the synthesis of extensive data: Bayesian statistics, structural equation modeling, and meta-analysis. The bulk of the workshop was the concurrent breakout groups, tasked with identifying opportunities for synthesis and collaboration across experimental forests and ranges. The four breakout topics were (1) vegetation composition, structure, and productivity; (2) water and vegetation management; (3) biomass for energy; and (4) climate change. Each breakout group discussed the tasks that should be implemented to advance synthesis on their topic area. Finally, on the last morning, there was a closeout session designed for sharing information from the breakout groups and furthering synthesis from EFRs.

Three very clear conclusions surfaced from this workshop:

1. Synthesis of vegetation and related data from EFRs is timely, scientifically relevant, challenging, and necessary.

2. We are hampered in our synthesis opportunities by an incomplete knowledge of what information and data are available, in what format, and from which EFRs.

3. Support for infrastructure of EFRs, in particular for data management, is a critical role for Forest Service Research and Development.

Outcomes from this workshop include the following:

- This workshop report, describing steps to advance synthesis across EFRs.

- Supporting Web content, useful for enhancing synthesis, on the national EFR Web site.

- A targeted workshop (to take place in the spring of 2010) to develop an understanding of stream nutrient variability (spatial and temporal) as an issue in developing nutrient criteria for water quality regulations.

- A directory of context for experimental watersheds, which will be a searchable, descriptive inventory of experimental watersheds within EFRs (available in early 2010).

- A metadatabase of vegetation-related studies on EFRs, including the following:

  - Developing a template for vegetation data sets that will facilitate sharing among EFRs.

  - Creating an expanded version of a summary table of treatments by EFR (available in late 2009).

In addition, the following needs for EFRs were identified. This list also represents one outcome of this workshop:

- A full-time national EFR manager/program leader position.

- Support for targeted workshops to encourage synthesis across EFRs.

- A Request for Proposals to fund cross-site research for EFRs every 3 years.

- Developing mechanisms for funding current and future synthesis products:

  - Bringing critical data sets into electronic format.

  - Support for infrastructure of EFRs.

- Outreach and education activities, including the following:

  - Getting national forest managers onto EFRs to encourage technology transfer.

  - Obtaining funding for writing nonscientific materials or outreach materials.

- Auditing all sites for consistency (technical work).

- Training for technical staff.

- Support to slow the loss of permanent positions, at both technical and research scientist levels, particularly from EFRs.

- Funding for postdocs and scholars (sabbaticals).

Introduction

The Forest Service Experimental Forests and Ranges (EFRs) were established initially to represent major forest vegetation types of the United States, to provide guidelines for management of those forests and ranges, and to serve as "outdoor classrooms" for land managers to learn how to better manage their forests. Research data collected during the 100 years since the first experimental forest was established in 1908 can be used synthetically to address regional and continental scale questions related to forest and range management, key forest ecosystem processes, wildlife habitat requirements, watershed management, and other topics.

A workshop was held September 29 to October 2, 2009, in Shepherdstown, WV, to advance our knowledge and ability to meet conservation challenges through the synthesis of long-term silviculture and range management research from EFRs. The focus of this inaugural workshop was on silviculture and range management research to showcase this vast, relatively unexplored synthesis opportunity. There will undoubtedly be other workshops, and numerous research products that follow on from this workshop, dealing with more synthesis opportunities. The purpose of this workshop was to plant the seeds among EFR researchers and develop direction.

Representatives from Forest Service EFRs and from our partner institutions met with the purpose of facilitating intersite data syntheses and analyses. The emphasis was on syntheses using existing long-term vegetation research data, with a focus on studies related to silviculture and range management experiments because those are the longest term studies on most of our EFRs.

West Virginia University (WVU) served as the workshop host because the WVU Division of Forestry and Natural Resources maintains a forest with long-term research studies and a long history of collaboration with the Fernow Experimental Forest and other Forest Service researchers. The purpose of the workshop was to review ongoing, nascent synthesis activities and to provoke and assist further synthesis activities among experimental forest researchers. The format included a 1-day plenary session with review of ongoing synthesis activities, followed by 1.5 days of breakout sessions for educational and synthetic activities.

This report describes some discussions and products of the workshop. The first part of this report includes papers and abstracts from some of the invited speakers, describing their experience with synthesis activities and using long-term or multisite data. Their experiences can provide inspiration and concrete recommendations for successful synthesis activities among EFRs. The second part of this report reflects the discussions from the breakout sessions. Avid participation by about 60 participants ensured the workshop's success. The appendix includes some of the more informal discussions and conversations. A Web site (under development) will be updated regularly to encourage continued discussion and further synthesis activities.

Part 1
Lessons Learned From Synthesis Activities

Silvicultural Research in the Douglas-Fir Region[1]

Robert O. Curtis[2] and Dean S. DeBell[3]

Abstract

This paper reviews the history of silvicultural research in the Douglas-fir region from circa 1900 to the present, emphasizing long-term studies that had a major influence on the development of Douglas-fir forestry. Silvicultural practices have evolved from the combination of formal research, observation and experience of managers, and changing social and economic conditions. Although much of the older work is unfamiliar to the present generation of foresters, it still has value and its history provides perspective on present problems and trends. This paper discusses recent changes in emphasis and experimental design.

Introduction

This brief history of Douglas-fir research in the coastal Pacific Northwest will emphasize long-term studies and their influence on the development of forest practices. It should remind us that silvicultural research is far from new, and that there is a large body of past work that is still relevant. The timber industry in the region began in the 1850s and soon became the dominant industry. In the early years, these were strictly liquidation operations, carried out without regard to the future.

Silvicultural research in the Douglas-fir region dates roughly from 1900. Initial work, mostly descriptive, began in the old Bureau of Forestry in the 1890s. The first published work was a series of monographs on the important timber species (e.g., Allen 1902, Frothingham 1909), based on field observation. It was early recognized that Douglas-fir was a moderately intolerant species and that most of the region's forests owed their origin and characteristics to periodic fires.

Silvicultural Systems and Regeneration

Long-term silvicultural research began with the 1908 arrival of Thornton Munger in the district forester's office in Portland, OR. He and others recognized that the most crucial, immediate problems were (1) fire protection and (2) regeneration methods. Munger undertook extensive measurements in existing second-growth stands, published the first volume and yield tables and much other information, and recommended "clean" cutting with retention of seed trees, followed by slash burning and protection from fire (Munger 1911). More elaborate silviculture was not feasible at that time.

Seed and nursery production research began at Wind River Nursery in 1911, initially by C.P. Willis and Julius Hofmann. The Wind River Experiment Station was established in 1913 (combined with the Division of Silvics in 1924 to form the present Pacific Northwest Research Station [PNW]). In 1915, a tract was set aside for experimental purposes; this tract was later greatly expanded in 1932 to form the present Wind River Experimental Forest. (Two other experimental forests on national forest land were established later: Cascade Head Experimental Forest on the Siuslaw National Forest in 1934, primarily for work with spruce and hemlock, and H.J. Andrews Experimental Forest on the Willamette National Forest in 1948.)

Julius Hofmann (director of the Wind River Experiment Station from 1913 to 1924) conducted extensive surveys of the distribution of regeneration on burned and logged areas. He established a series of plots along extensive transects in then unstocked areas; remeasurements in later years documented gradual restocking by seed windborne over long distances. He also established the first precommercial thinning study in the region in 1920, was the first to link humidity and fire risk, and worked with Munger on the early heredity trials.

Leo Isaac began work in 1924 and devoted most of his working life to the problems of natural regeneration. He became the lead-

[1] This is a minor revision of a paper given at the Society of American Foresters Convention, Portland, OR, Oct 24, 2007

[2] Emeritus Scientist, U S Department of Agriculture (USDA) Forest Service, Pacific Northwest Research Station, Olympia, WA

[3] Research Forester (retired), USDA Forest Service, Pacific Northwest Research Station, Olympia, WA

ing authority on Douglas-fir regeneration (Isaac 1943) and was an early advocate of tree improvement programs in the 1950s.

Abortive efforts at "selective timber management" in the 1930s (Curtis 1998, Isaac 1956, Kirkland and Brandstrom 1936) led many to conclude that there was no alternative to clearcutting. In the 1940s, there was general adoption of dispersed moderate-sized clearcuts, first with natural regeneration and later with planting. The clearcut/burn/plant regime was highly successful for a timber production goal and was almost universal until the 1990s. Most silvicultural research was devoted to refining the system, although there were a few trials of shelterwood on problem sites.

In the early 1950s, PNW and Oregon State University (OSU) began extensive work on the control of shrub competition. This work was later concentrated at OSU and continues to the present. In recent years, environmental concerns, public pressures, and endangered species considerations have revived interest in alternative silvicultural systems, and these issues are a major aspect of current silvicultural research. These alternatives involve a wider range of species, harvest methods, silvicultural systems, management regimes, and regeneration methods (e.g., Curtis et al. 1998).

Stand Density Control

Plantation Spacing
Leo Isaac established a Douglas-fir plantation spacing test at Wind River Experiment Station in 1925, on a relatively poor site. This spacing test was remeasured at intervals through 1990 (Miller et al. 2004, Reukema 1979). Results showed that the 10- by 10-ft and 12- by 12-ft (3- by 3-m and 3.7- by 3.7-m) spacings were markedly superior to the close spacings and led owners to abandon the close spacing that had been the prevailing practice.

The University of British Columbia established a series of spacing trials in 1957 and following years on an excellent site, with generally similar results (Reukema and Smith 1987). In the 1960s, additional trials were established by several companies and by the British Columbia Ministry of Forests, and, in 1980, a much more extensive trial using five species was established at Wind River Experimental Forest. There was also some use of the Nelder design in spacing trials by the

University of British Columbia, Washington Department of Natural Resources, and OSU, although most of these trials have never been published. All these trials showed markedly greater diameter growth at wide spacings. Some showed effects on height growth, mostly on poor sites.

Thinning Research: Pre-World War II (WWII)
Thinning was long regarded as impractical under northwest conditions because of the low value of small material and the abundant supply of large timber. Despite the prevailing opinion of thinning, a number of—at the time—visionary studies were established in the 1920 to 1940 period. In 1920, Hofmann established a precommercial thinning trial in a 9-year-old stand at the Wind River Experiment Station. Walter Meyer established an additional trial in 1933, thinned at ages 31 and 50. The Schenstrom thinning plots on Vancouver Island were established in 1929 in an 18-year-old stand on an excellent site. These plots have been thinned repeatedly, although the originally planned differences in treatments were more or less lost. The Mt. Walker thinning study was established in a 60-year-old poor site stand on the Olympic National Forest from 1934 to 1937. Response was poor in the early years, but, when remeasured in 1991, the thinned plots were in excellent condition and had not reached peak mean annual increment despite their age (Curtis 1998).

Thinning Research: Post-WWII to Present
In addition to earlier trials in Douglas-fir, two extensive pre-commercial thinning trials were installed in hemlock at Cascade Head, OR, and Clallam Bay, WA, in 1963 and 1971, respectively (Hoyer and Swanzey 1986). These trials showed striking response. Trials and observation of existing young stands showed that many young stands were too dense for optimum growth and resistance to wind and snow breakage. With the changed economic outlook that followed WWII, precommercial thinning became common from the late 1960s onward.

Interest in commercial thinning was stimulated by the economic revival after WWII, the increasing acreage of second-growth stands, and the foreseeable end of old-growth timber. The PNW undertook several operational-scale commercial thinning experiments on industrial lands, under cooperative agreements with landowners. Three experimental forests were established for the primary purpose of thinning research: the Hemlock Experimental Forest near Hoquiam, WA; the Voight Creek Experimental Forest near Orting, WA; and the McCleary

Experimental Forest near McCleary, WA. These forests were midage, previously unmanaged stands of natural origin. Repeated thinnings included different thinning cycles. Growth and mortality were measured over a period of about 20 years.

Results showed some increase in diameter growth and reduced mortality but little or no volume gain from thinning in these midage, previously untreated stands (Reukema 1972, Reukema and Pienaar 1973). Together with higher logging costs and the continued availability of mature timber, these results markedly dampened interest in commercial thinning. Concurrently, a number of industrial owners established other thinning studies. Most have not been published. Two long-term studies in older stands (e.g., Williamson 1982) found little difference in gross volume growth but a large reduction in mortality on thinned plots. Allen Berg of OSU established an extensive series of thinning trials in the 1950s. These trials have had considerable use as demonstration areas, but no formal report has ever been published. Most of these studies were begun comparatively late, after extensive crown reduction had occurred. The marked differences between initially overstocked stands and those established with early spacing control showed the need for thinning experiments begun at much younger ages. Several large-scale regional studies attempted to address these and related concerns.

The cooperative Levels-of-Growing-Stock (LOGS) study in Douglas-fir was conducted jointly by several organizations (Curtis et al. 1997). Begun in 1961, it was installed in stands in the precommercial thinning stage and included a wide range of sites. Nine installations followed a common design originated by George Staebler and Richard Williamson, consisting of 27 plots with 3 replicates of 8 thinning treatments plus control. Principal results included the following:

- Gross volume increment was greatest at the highest growing stock levels, contrary to a belief widely held at the time the study was initiated.

- Volume increment was much more closely related to growing stock level than was basal area increment.

- Net volume increment of unthinned controls exceeded that of thinned plots, although there are indications that the relationship may be reversing with advancing age.

- All thinning treatments markedly increased diameter growth and had striking effects on understory composition and development.

The Stand Management Cooperative (SMC) is a large cooperative effort headquartered at the University of Washington (Chappell et al. 1987). Its formation in 1985 stemmed from the realization that existing data (1) did not provide adequate coverage of young stands with early density control, (2) did not cover a sufficient range of initial plantation spacings, and (3) were often of poor quality and inconsistent in measurement standards. SMC involves many larger landowners and uses standardized design and measurement procedures. Its activities include work on timber quality and fertilization as well as work on stocking control per se. The data are rapidly becoming the major source of information on young stand development of Douglas-fir and western hemlock. The Hardwood Management Cooperative at OSU is a somewhat similar but smaller program.

Forest Fertilization and Long-Term Site Productivity

Stimulation of tree growth by added nitrogen was first demonstrated in the late 1940s. Several organizations began research on forest fertilization (Chappell et al. 1992). The Regional Forest Nutrition Research Project was established in 1969 under the leadership of Stanley Gessel of the University of Washington. This initiative was a cooperative program (that has since merged with SMC) financed by many major landowners in the region. Over the years, this program established a very extensive series of long-term field trials that are now the principal source of information on the subject. In general, results showed that Douglas-fir response to nitrogen (N) is inversely related to site index and is greater in combination with density control. N fertilization is a widely adopted practice on industrial lands and some State lands. Response to nutrients other than N has been highly variable. Response of hemlock to N fertilization has also been erratic.

It has often been hypothesized that soil compaction and the removal of nutrients and organic matter associated with timber harvest may reduce site productivity. Attempts to examine the question by retrospective studies have yielded no clear generalizations. There are two major ongoing long-term experiments in the Pacific Northwest that attempt to address the question: (1) the Long-Term Ecosystem Productivity Study and (2) the Long-Term Site Productivity (LTSP) Study. These studies are affiliates of the National Long-Term Soil Productivity Study

(Powers et al. 2005) but differ considerably from that study and from each other in design and component treatments. Treatments are replicated within each of several installations in each study. Both studies are still in the early stages and many years will be required for conclusive results, although some preliminary results from one installation of the LTSP study are available (Ares et al. 2007).

Tree Improvement

In 1912, Munger established the Douglas-Fir Heredity Study, a pioneering provenance trial maintained until 1993, which clearly demonstrated the importance of seed source. He also established the Wind River Arboretum as a long-term trial of exotic species. Although some exotics showed initial promise, their long-term survival and growth proved far inferior to the native species.

From 1950 to the 1960s, several programs in tree improvement were established. John Duffield and Roy Silen were prominent in the early work. Several tree improvement cooperatives have been established. Additional provenance trials were established, seed collection zones were defined, breeding programs were undertaken, and a large number of field trials were established. This work continues.

Growth and Yield Research

In 1910, Munger began a program of establishing permanent growth plots in second-growth stands, which continued until 1940 (Williamson 1963) and formed the basis for a number of publications over the years.

In 1930, McArdle and Meyer published an elaborate normal yield table for Douglas-fir (McArdle and Meyer 1930), which had a great influence. The yield table served for half a century as *the* guide to stand development and management planning (Curtis and Marshall 2004). Like all normal yield tables, however, it represented well-stocked natural unmanaged stands and could not provide the information needed for intensive management.

Staebler combined McArdle's net yield table with mortality data from the permanent plot series begun by Munger and developed estimates of gross yield. He then used these estimates to produce estimates for thinned stands under the then-current assumption that gross yield would be little affected by differences in stocking (Staebler 1960). These estimates represent an early example of stand simulation (albeit not computerized). Staebler recognized that the hypothesized constant gross increment over a range of stocking had never been demonstrated for Douglas-fir, and that existing data did not cover a wide range of stocking and did not allow a test of this hypothesis. He went on to design the LOGS study referred to previously.

Following WWII, a number of organizations (including major industrial landowners) began installing permanent plots. By the 1970s, a large number of permanent plots were in existence, including natural unmanaged stands, some fertilized stands, thinned stands, and some young plantations. The advent of the computer made it possible to handle large amounts of data and to construct stand simulators that summarized the results of many studies. There were efforts to assemble existing data and construct simulation programs that could produce estimates of stand development under a variety of management regimes (e.g., Curtis et al.1981).

It quickly became apparent that, although large quantities of remeasured plot data existed and although some data from work begun before the war covered quite long periods of time, there were major limitations on its usefulness. The data were not well distributed geographically, were primarily from stands of natural origin without early stocking control, and did not include extreme treatments. A considerable part of the existing data was of little value because of inconsistent measurement standards and procedures, poor quality control, inadequate documentation, and frequent use of excessively small plots.

These deficiencies led to the establishment of the SMC (referred to previously) and to associated efforts to improve long-term experimental plot procedures. Efforts to improve simulation programs continue. These programs provide the best means of summarizing the results of the numerous existing silvicultural experiments. The objective is a suite of models that can integrate the results of all aspects of silvicultural research into a coherent framework for predicting stand dynamics, treatment response, and forest productivity.

Changes in Experimental Designs

Early (pre-WWII) field experiments commonly used large plots (0.5 to 1.0 acre), usually without replication or randomization. Statistical designs were introduced from agriculture in the late 1930s. Following WWII, many but not all field studies were designed for statistical analysis, with replication and randomization. The scarcity of uniform areas that could accommodate the necessary numbers of plots, plus cost considerations, led many researchers to use quite small plots—often 1/10 acre and sometimes as small as 1/20 acre. This practice severely limited the usefulness of the data for many purposes and made the extension of results to larger and more heterogeneous areas problematic. In recent years, the problems associated with very small plots have been commonly recognized.

Social Change and Silvicultural Objectives

Until quite recently, most silvicultural research was directed at timber production as the major objective. For some 40 years after WWII, the standard regime was to clearcut, burn, and plant, usually to Douglas-fir, with or without later thinning. There was a progressive reduction in rotations, while the replacement of natural regeneration by planting eliminated the need to limit the size of clearcuts. The result was large areas in the unsightly early regeneration stage, with most of the remainder in uniform young stands that much of the public regarded as not particularly attractive and that are the least productive condition for wildlife. These factors combined with widespread urbanization and the associated rise of the environmental movement to produce conflicts between public perceptions and attitudes versus economic objectives, with associated constraints on management. These conflicts are the most serious forestry problem we have in the Northwest today.

There are now considerable differences in objectives among public, industrial, and small private owners. Much current silvicultural research is concerned with efforts to minimize conflicts between diverse resource management goals, economics, and social considerations that include public attitudes and various legal constraints such as the National Environmental Policy Act, Endangered Species Act, and State forest practice rules. This work includes efforts to develop stand structures with some of the characteristics found in old-growth forests.

In addition, defining relationships between increment, growing stock, management regimes, and rotations seems pertinent to current concerns about global warming and carbon sequestration. Douglas-fir is a long-lived species that maintains good growth to advanced ages and lends itself to a variety of management strategies and objectives (Curtis and Carey 1996).

There is also much interest in wildlife habitat, biodiversity concerns, and scenic effects that cannot be evaluated on small plots. This interest has led to a number of long-term studies using large, operational-scale treatment units (Poage and Anderson 2007) on the order of 20 to 80 acres. Compared to traditional small-plot studies, they have major advantages and major disadvantages, including the following.

Advantages:

- Results are representative of the real world, without the uncertainties involved in applying results from highly selected small plots to the more heterogeneous conditions that managers must deal with.

- Large treatment units make it possible to evaluate a variety of response variables, in addition to the traditional variables of stand and tree volume and increment. These variables include the following:

  • Visual effects and public perceptions.

  • Wildlife habitat.

  • Harvesting costs.

  • Economic returns.

  • Biodiversity.

- Large treatment units are extremely valuable as demonstration areas, where forest managers and interested segments of the public can see the results of alternative management regimes.

Disadvantages:

- Large treatment units are expensive to install and maintain.

- They are dependent on common interests and continued close cooperation between research and land management organizations.

- They require continuity in personnel and funding.

- The scarcity of reasonably homogeneous areas of sufficient size to accommodate such studies limits the number of treatments that can be included and the possible number of replications.

- The greater inherent variability within and between treatment areas reduces the power of statistical tests.

- Over a long timeframe, serious disruptions are likely to arise from weather events, insect infestations, and political factors.

These studies are generally joint efforts between a land management organization(s) and a research organization(s). (As an example, our Silvicultural Options Study at Olympia is a joint effort of the Washington Department of Natural Resources [the land manager], PNW, and the University of Washington, with Canadian replications installed and maintained by the British Columbia Ministry of Forests). Joint responsibility provides facilities and expertise not otherwise available and helps cushion the fluctuations in funding and priorities that occur within individual organizations. There are considerable differences in design and emphasis among the existing studies that reflect the particular interests and priorities of the designers. These differences frequently offer opportunities for superimposed supplementary studies, given the necessary personnel and funding.

Conclusions

Most past research has been on Douglas-fir, the economically most important species in the region. Secondary species (hemlock, true firs, and hardwoods) are also important economically and ecologically, and a lesser but increasing amount of research has been done on these species. In the early years, most silvicultural research was conducted by the Forest Service on Forest Service lands, much of it on dedicated experimental forests such as Wind River. Much of our research is now conducted on State or private lands, as cooperative efforts of PNW, the universities, and industrial owners. This shift is partly a matter of efficiency in using sources of funding and expertise. It also is partly a result of changing national forest policies and priorities. The Northwest Forest Plan effectively halted manipulative silvicultural studies on the long-established Wind River and Cascade Head Experimental Forests, although we are still remeasuring some existing studies. Reduced staffing and changing priorities have sharply reduced National Forest System capabilities and interest, and managers are reluctant

or unable to allow treatments that might arouse opposition or that conflict with established guidelines. The sales and appeals process can involve lengthy delays. All these factors can disrupt schedules and experimental designs.

Formal silvicultural research in the Douglas-fir region can be roughly divided into three periods with differing emphases:

1. 1908 to circa 1945: Primary research emphasis was on the regeneration of logged areas and unstocked burns and on yield tables; research was also begun on thinning. Most research was conducted by the Forest Service.

2. 1945 to circa 1990: Research emphasis was on questions and practices directly related to timber production. There was a shift to intensive silviculture in the 1960s, with a concomitant expansion in research. The universities assumed a major role. Several companies (Weyerhaeuser, Crown Zellerbach, MacMillan-Bloedel) developed strong in-house research programs.

3. Circa 1990 to present: Research aimed at timber production as a primary goal is deemphasized by the Federal agencies. The primary emphasis of public agencies is now on environmental, scenic, and biodiversity goals, with efforts to reconcile these goals with some level of timber production. Funding for Forest Service silvicultural research of any sort progressively declined. In-house industrial research declined sharply (partly because of reorganizations and timber land divestitures by several large companies), although it was replaced in part by various landowner-supported research cooperatives (usually at universities).

The Douglas-fir region has a long history of long-term silvicultural observation and experimentation. Much of our present knowledge is derived from this work. Data from these experiments have often been found useful for a variety of purposes, in addition to those purposes envisioned at the time the experiments were established. Experience has shown that ultimate conclusions from long-term experiments can be considerably different from initial indications, and that objectives and available techniques can be expected to change over time.

This has been a very sketchy account of a large subject. Much more thorough presentations are available in Curtis et al. (2007) and Herring and Greene (2007).

Literature Cited

Allen, E.T. 1902. Western hemlock. Bull. 13. Washington, DC: U.S. Department of Agriculture, Bureau of Forestry. 55 p.

Ares, A.; Terry, T.A.; Piatek, K.B., et al. 2007. The Fall River long-term site productivity study: site characteristics, methods, and biomass and carbon and nitrogen stores before and after harvest. Gen. Tech. Rep. PNW-GTR-691. Portland, OR: U.S. Department of Agriculture, Forest Service, Pacific Northwest Research Station. 85 p.

Chappell, H.N.; Curtis, R.O.; Hyink, D.M.; Maguire, D.A. 1987. The Pacific Northwest stand management cooperative and its field installation design. In: Ek, A.R.; Shifley, S.R.; Burk, T.E., eds. Forest growth modelling and prediction. Gen. Tech. Rep. NC-120. St. Paul, MN: U.S. Department of Agriculture, Forest Service, North Central Forest Experiment Station: Vol. 1: 1073–1080.

Chappell, H.N.; Omule, S.A.Y.; Gessel, S.P. 1992. Fertilization in coastal northwest forests: using response information in developing stand-level tactics. In: Chappell, H.N.; Weetman, G.F.; Miller, R.E., eds. Forest fertilization: sustaining and improving nutrition and growth of western forests. Institute of Forest Resources contribution No. 73. Seattle, WA: University of Washington, College of Forest Resources, Institute of Forest Resources: 98–113.

Curtis, R.O. 1998. "Selective cutting" in Douglas-fir: history revisited. Journal of Forestry. 96(7): 40–46.

Curtis, R.O.; Carey, A.B. 1996. Timber supply in the Pacific Northwest: managing for economic and ecological values in the Pacific Northwest. Journal of Forestry. 94: 4–7.

Curtis, R.O.; Clendenen, G.W.; DeMars, D.J. 1981. A new stand simulator for coast Douglas-fir: DFSIM user's guide. Gen. Tech. Rep. PNW-128. Portland, OR: U.S. Department of Agriculture, Forest Service, Pacific Northwest Forest and Range Experiment Station. 79 p.

Curtis, R.O.; DeBell, D.S.; Harrington, C.A., et al. 1998. Silviculture for multiple objectives in the Douglas-fir region. Gen. Tech. Rep. PNW-GTR-435. Portland, OR: U.S. Department of Agriculture, Forest Service, Pacific Northwest Research Station. 123 p.

Curtis, R.O.; DeBell, D.S.; Miller, R.E., et al. 2007. Silvicultural research and the evolution of forest practices in the Douglas-fir region. Gen. Tech. Rep. PNW-GTR-696. Portland, OR: U.S. Department of Agriculture, Forest Service, Pacific Northwest Research Station. 172 p.

Curtis, R.O.; Marshall, D.D. 2004. Douglas-fir growth and yield: research 1909–1960. Western Journal of Applied Forestry. 19(1): 66–68.

Curtis, R.O.; Marshall, D.D.; Bell, J.F. 1997. LOGS: a pioneering example of silvicultural research in coast Douglas-fir. Journal of Forestry. 95(7): 19–25.

Frothingham, E.H. 1909. Douglas fir: a study of the Pacific Coast and Rocky Mountain forms. Circ. 150. Washington, DC: U.S. Department of Agriculture, Forest Service. 38 p.

Herring, M.; Greene, S. 2007. Forest of time—a century of science at Wind River Experimental Forest. Corvallis, OR: Oregon State University Press. 188 p.

Hoyer, G.E.; Swanzey, J.D. 1986. Growth and yield of western hemlock in the Pacific Northwest following thinning near the time of initial crown closing. Res. Pap. PNW-365. Portland, OR: U.S Department of Agriculture, Forest Service, Pacific Northwest Research Station. 52 p.

Isaac, L.A. 1943. Reproductive habits of Douglas-fir. Washington, DC: Charles Lathrop Pack Forestry Foundation. 107 p.

Isaac, L.A. 1956. Place of partial cutting in old-growth stands of the Douglas-fir region. Res. Pap. PNW-RP-16. Portland, OR: U.S. Department of Agriculture, Forest Service, Pacific Northwest Forest and Range Experiment Station. 48 p.

Kirkland, B.P.; Brandstrom, A.J.E. 1936. Selective timber management in the Douglas-fir region. Washington, DC: U.S. Department of Agriculture, Forest Service. 122 p.

McArdle, R.E.; Meyer, W.H. 1930. The yield of Douglas fir in the Pacific Northwest. Tech. Bull. 201. Washington, DC: U.S. Department of Agriculture, Forest Service. 64 p.

Miller, R.E.; Reukema, D.; Anderson, H.W. 2004. Tree growth and soil relations at the 1925 Wind River spacing test in coast Douglas-fir. Res. Pap. PNW-RP-558. Portland, OR: U.S. Department of Agriculture, Forest Service, Pacific Northwest Research Station. 41 p.

Munger, T.T. 1911. The growth and management of Douglas-fir in the Pacific Northwest. Circ. 175. Washington, DC: U.S. Department of Agriculture, Forest Service. 27 p.

Poage, N.J.; Anderson, P.D. 2007. Large-scale silviculture experiments of western Oregon and Washington. Gen. Tech. Rep. PNW-GTR-713. Portland, OR: U.S. Department of Agriculture, Forest Service, Pacific Northwest Research Station. 44 p.

Powers, R.E.; Scott, D.A.; Sanchez, F.G., et al. 2005. The North American long term soil productivity experiment: findings from the first decade of research. Forest Ecology and Management. 220: 31–50.

Reukema, D.L. 1972. Twenty-one-year development of Douglas-fir stands repeatedly thinned at varying intervals. Res. Pap. PNW-141. Portland, OR: U.S. Department of Agriculture, Forest Service, Pacific Northwest Forest and Range Experiment Station. 23 p.

Reukema, D.L. 1979. Fifty-year development of Douglas-fir stands planted at various spacings. Res. Pap. PNW-253. Portland, OR: U.S. Department of Agriculture, Forest Service, Pacific Northwest Forest and Range Experiment Station. 21 p.

Reukema, D.L.; Pienaar, L.V. 1973. Yields with and without repeated commercial thinnings in a high-site-quality Douglas-fir stand. Res. Pap. PNW-155. Portland, OR: U.S. Department of Agriculture, Forest Service, Pacific Northwest Forest and Range Experiment Station. 15 p.

Reukema, D.L.; Smith, J.H.G. 1987. Development over 25 years of Douglas-fir, western hemlock, and western redcedar planted at various spacings on a very good site in British Columbia. Res. Pap. PNW-RP-381. Portland, OR: U.S. Department of Agriculture, Forest Service, Pacific Northwest Forest and Range Experiment Station. 45 p.

Staebler, G.R. 1960. Theoretical derivation of numerical thinning schedules for Douglas-fir. Forest Science. 6(2): 98–109.

Williamson, R.L. 1963. Growth and yield records from well-stocked stands of Douglas-fir. Res. Pap. PNW-4. Portland, OR: U.S. Department of Agriculture, Forest Service, Pacific Northwest Forest and Range Experiment Station. 24 p.

Williamson, R.L. 1982. Response to commercial thinning in a 110-year-old Douglas-fir stand. Res. Pap. PNW-296. Portland, OR: U.S. Department of Agriculture, Forest Service, Pacific Northwest Forest and Range Experiment Station. 16 p.

Additional Reading

Hann, D.W.; Hester, A.S.; Olsen, C.L. 1997. ORGANON user's manual. Version 6.0. Corvallis, OR: Oregon State University, Department of Forest Resources. 167 p.

Experimental Forests and Ranges as a Network for Long-Term Data

Martin Vavra[1] and John Mitchell[2]

Abstract

In the new millennium, national leaders and policymakers are facing profound issues regarding people and the environment. Experimental Forests and Ranges (EFRs), managed by the Forest Service, U.S. Department of Agriculture (USDA), form a network of locations amenable to the development of long-term data collection across many major ecosystems of the continental United States, Alaska, and Hawaii. Truly long-term data sets dealing with range and grasslands are rare but do exist. Unfortunately, the status of older studies, in terms of longevity and variables monitored, are incompletely documented. The paucity of long-term data sets is related to personnel turnovers and a lack of ownership of long-term studies that may be sampled only every 5 or 10 years, coupled with limited funds available to hire personnel for data collection. Any long-term monitoring program should start with the basics of seasonal and daily precipitation and daily maximum and minimum temperatures. Change in plant species composition is an important indicator of the integrity of the plant association. Photographs can be taken at permanent points to qualitatively measure how vegetation changes over time, for the detection of changes in vegetation structure and for visually documenting vegetation change. To successfully provide long-term biotic and abiotic data that can support broad-scale research into contemporary issues, such as climate change, species invasions, desertification, and fire, these EFRs must be connected in a network.

Introduction

In the new millennium, national leaders and policymakers are facing profound issues regarding people and the environment.

Among these are impacts of climate change and the value of ecosystem services. A more complete understanding of these and other issues have been shown to benefit from the analysis of long-term vegetation data sets (Swetnam et al. 1999). Both issues point out the need for collecting and maintaining long-term data. Climate change and the need for planning to adapt to it have brought particularly sharp focus on the lack of available data (Powledge 2008).

EFRs, managed by the Forest Service, form a network of locations amenable to the development of long-term data collection across many major ecosystems of the continental United States, Alaska, and Hawaii (Lugo et al. 2006). Historically, long-term data collection on range sites encompassed a 10- to 15-year period and involved different intensities of livestock grazing. Common variables included weather information, plant production, composition changes related to grazing intensity (including exclusion of grazing), and livestock gains (Klipple and Costello 1960, Martin and Cable 1974, Skovlin et al. 1976) (fig. 1).

The objectives of this paper are to (1) review the status of long-term data collection on experimental ranges and experimental

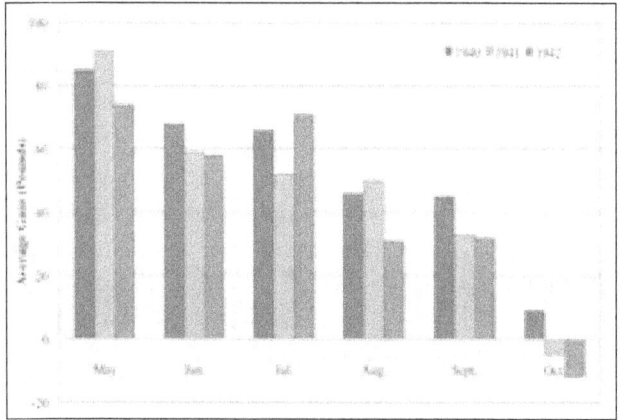

Figure 1.—*Average monthly cattle weight gains (in pounds) at the Central Plains Experimental Range, Nunn, CO (taken from Johnson 1953).*

[1] Supervisory Rangeland Scientist, U S Department of Agriculture (USDA) Forest Service, Pacific Northwest Research Station, La Grande, OR
[2] Rangeland Scientist (retired), USDA Forest Service, Rocky Mountain Research Station, Fort Collins, CO

forests that incorporate rangelands and (2) suggest a rationale for using these ranges and forests as a network to monitor driving variables needed to test and validate models that describe how disturbances like climate change, fire, and grazing affect ecosystem processes.

Status of Long-Term Data

Truly long-term data sets (20+ years) are rare but do exist. Studies examining successional trends on a few experimental ranges have been exceptions (Angel and McClaran 2001, Buffington and Herbel 1965). Unfortunately, the status of older studies, in terms of longevity and variables monitored, are incompletely documented. Their records may be boxed and archived in warehouses and other locations generally inaccessible to scientists today (Oakes 2008).

Pearson et al. (2008) reported on grazing and excluded plots at the Fort Valley Experimental Forest in Arizona that were sampled from 1912 to 1941 and rediscovered and resampled from 1996 to 2007. Johnson (2003) described 90 years of plant succession on green fescue (*Festuca viridula* Vasey) grasslands in the subalpine ecological zone of the Wallowa Mountains in Oregon, where changes in sheep grazing management over time resulted in dramatic changes in plant community composition (fig. 2). Gibbens and Beck (1988) reported on long-term plots that were established between 1915 and 1932, continuously evaluated until 1947, and only a portion evaluated annually until 1979, when data collection was discontinued.

A number of reasons have likely contributed to the scarcity of long-term data sets. Universities, which undertake much of the natural resource-related research, tend to receive support for short-term studies because the university reward system promotes research leading to frequent publications (Kasten 1984). Federal research agencies, alternatively, commonly focus their work on longer term projects that are tied to experimental areas (Klade 2006). Personnel turnovers and a lack of ownership of long-term studies that may be sampled only every 5 or 10 years, coupled with limited funds available to hire personnel for data collection, are also likely root causes.

Another shortcoming of some long-term data sets with infrequent monitoring is the lack of concomitant weather and soils statistics (Mueggler 1992). Sharp et al. (1990) pictori-

ally demonstrated the link that growing season and annual precipitation have on species composition and productivity on a research site in southern Idaho (fig. 3).

Powledge (2008) described a Government Accountability Office report and other assessments that concluded that the Federal land management agencies have been lax in inventorying and monitoring the resources they control. At a national scale, however, the Forest Inventory and Analysis (FIA) program of the Forest Service maintains a data bank on thousands of forest plots across the United States (Frayer and Furnival 1999). FIA plots found on nonforested sites, including rangeland, are not currently sampled. Similarly, the USDA Natural Resources Conservation Service monitors resource information as part of its National Resources Inventory (NRI) (Nusser and Goebel 1997). NRI plots are currently sampled only on non-Federal lands. Thus, U.S. rangelands managed by Federal agencies are effectively unmonitored at a national scale.

Figure 2.—*Permanent photo point of a green fescue plant community in the Wallowa Mountains in 1907 and 1993. The 1993 photo depicts recovery from sheep grazing (Johnson 2003).*

Figure 3.—*Permanent photo transect near the Lee A. Sharp Experimental Area, Raft River Valley, ID. In 1964, spring precipitation was more than twice the normal amount of approximately 10 cm. In 1972, spring precipitation was less than one-half the normal amount. Photos courtesy of the University of Idaho (Sharp et al. 1990).*

Development of Long-Term Monitoring

After the decision has been made to initiate long-term data collection, the issues of what to collect and who will collect it must be addressed. Data collection has historically been justified by and associated with individual research studies; however, Forest Service research studies, based on problem analyses that are systematically reviewed and revised over time, do not lend themselves to collecting and archiving consistent data across broader timeframes. The basis and funding for long-term monitoring on EFRs should logically be tied to mechanisms that maintain these sites. The monitoring issue is complicated by the need to collect statistically valid data for a reasonable cost of money and time. An overarching goal of monitoring plant community dynamics is to sample adequately to identify trends and be able to differentiate them from normal fluctuations (Miles 1979) (fig. 4).

Scale becomes an important consideration given the large potential network of EFRs and common data collection. The extent, grain, and frequency of observations must be commensurate with the scale of the ecosystem being observed (Allen and Hoekstra 1992). At a national scale, indicators are more general and are not tied to individual species or soil series (Mitchell 2000), while indicators at the management unit scale track ecological processes taking place at plant community and landscape levels. For example, ecosystem health at a regional level might be defined in terms of invasive and woody plants, fragmentation of the rangeland base, and the ecological footprint of livestock grazing (Asner et al. 2004), while at the local level land health is often described in terms of species composition and detailed soil information (Pyke et al. 2002).

Scale is not the only issue of concern in long-term monitoring. Research has shown that vegetation response to climate change is a function of temperature, water availability, nitrogen concentration, and atmospheric carbon dioxide (CO_2) composition;

Figure 4.—*Bunchgrass range on the Manitou Experimental Forest in fair ecological condition, unknown date in early 1940s. Early rangeland monitoring research often focused on understanding the species composition of different condition classes and how they changed over time (taken from Costello and Schwan 1946).*

however, to be useful in parameterizing models, these abiotic variables must be monitored simultaneously (Morgan et al. 2004, Owensby et al. 1999) (table 1). Concurrent monitoring of biotic and abiotic variables also is required to assess long-term responses to other disturbance factors.

One approach in selecting a long-term sampling protocol is to frame it within the concept of ecosystem services. Ecosystem services are the ecological functions that sustain and improve human life (Daily 1997). These functions have been broken into four different categories by the Millennium Ecosystem Assessment (2005): provisioning services, regulating services, cultural services, and supporting services. Provisioning services are identified by such entities as food, fiber, and water. Cultural services serve the spiritual well-being of humans and include recreation, heritage values, and education. Regulating services are air quality, climate, erosion, water management, and carbon sequestration. Primary production, soil formation, and nutrient cycling are defined as support services. Describing trends as changes in ecological services is a better illustration for the general public than more technical descriptors of ecosystem attributes.

In general, the dynamics of carbon sequestration in rangeland ecosystems are substantially less than for forests and croplands, even though U.S. rangelands contain up to 21 billion metric tons of carbon within the top 2 m of soil (Follett 2001). Negra et al. (2008) reported that, on rangelands not managed by the U.S. Federal Government—which tend to be the most productive rangelands (Talbert et al. 2007)—little measurable change of soil carbon or carbon density took place. Nonetheless, with increasing interest in tracking CO_2 to spatially identify global sources and sinks (Crisp and Johnson 2005), establishing long-term carbon data from rangelands to provide key information to the total carbon budget is of obvious importance.

Climatic and soil factors, specifically precipitation and temperature, are the main drivers in determining plant associations and their productivity (Humphrey 1962). Any long-term monitoring program should start with the basics of seasonal and daily precipitation, and daily maximum and minimum temperatures. Gibbens and Beck (1988) concluded that long-term detailed studies of desert vegetation receiving precipitation from localized convectional storms should not be undertaken unless precipitation can be measured at each sampling site. Soil water and temperature should be considered at the onset of the growing season.

Concomitant with temperature, precipitation, and soil water data, measures of net primary productivity (NPP) should also be made. Although difficult to measure because of inherent spatial and temporal variation (Herrick *at el.* 2005), NPP is an ecosystem process important to the management and quantification of ecosystem services.

Change in plant species composition is an important indicator of the integrity of the plant association (Pellant et al. 2000). In addition, changing species composition may provide the evidence of shifts in species in response to climate change (Lenoir et al. 2008). Species composition of plant communities is the standard measurement that identifies whether successional changes have occurred or are occurring. Various metrics, including biomass, density, frequency, and cover, are commonly used to evaluate changes in species composition of communities (Holechek et al. 1998). Choice of methodology is usually based on accuracy and ease of sampling with the consideration that, over time, different people will be sampling. In general, a two-dimensional variable (cover) is less variable and easier to accurately estimate than a three-dimensional variable (biomass) (Bonham 1989). If accurate estimates of NPP are needed, however, it may be beneficial to base species composition on biomass. Plant community composition can be

Table 1.—*Species percent cover over time on a green fescue grassland in the Wallowa Mountains (Johnson 2003).*

Species and ground condition	1938	1953	1959	1999
Green fescue	68	53	56	82
Western needlegrass	0	46	43	18
Ross' sedge	0	0	0	1
Hoary velvet lupine	32	0	0	0
Bare ground	NA	17	24	10
Erosion pavement	NA	9	8	7

NA = no data available.

related to the several ecosystem services, including watershed integrity and the incidence of invasive species.

An additional characteristic of interest in plant communities is that of plant phenology; however, sampling should be comprehensive enough to cover several species across life forms and all stages of phenology (Post et al. 2008). These authors reported that different species' phenological events responded differently to climate change. It was suggested that sampling include emergence, flower bud set, blooming, and fruit set. The use of indicator species to detect phenological shifts due to climate has been proposed; however, long-term data sets are needed to isolate the effects of climate from other disturbance factors (Miller-Rushing and Primack 2008). Alternatively, emerging methodologies of landscape phenology appear promising as a mechanism to monitor phenology at a scale more useful to detect responses to climate change.

Photographs can be taken at permanent points to qualitatively measure how vegetation changes over time, for the detection of changes in vegetation structure, and for visually documenting vegetation change (Herrick et al. 2005). Hall (2002), in a discussion of repeat photography methodology, illustrated streamside changes, riparian willow response to beavers, logging, livestock use, and mountain pine beetle kill of lodgepole pine (*Pinus contorta* var. *latifolia* Englm.) as examples of useful documentation of vegetation change. Skovlin and Thomas (1995) used repeat photography to interpret long-term vegetation trends in the mountains of northeastern Oregon. Original photos were all taken before 1925 and the last in 1992. In some locations, photos were also taken in the 1960s, 1970s, and 1980s. Skovlin and Thomas (1995) noted that, over a timeframe of that length (minimum of 67 years), interpretation of plant composition changes was not simple. Composition change could have been the result of weather, ungulate grazing, fire, insects or disease, rodents, other agents, or combinations of the aforementioned factors (Skovlin and Thomas 1995). Obviously, if only repeat photography is the sampling agent, the best-case sampling occurs in a timeframe in which disturbance events can be recorded as supplementary material to aid in interpretation. Despite these limitations, repeat photography is an excellent complement to climate and vegetation sampling previously described.

Further complicating the development of long-term vegetation sampling protocols is the issue of herbivory. Herbivory has been recognized as a chronic disturbance agent (Augustine and McNaughton 1998, Hobbs 1996, Riggs et al. 2000). Herbivory, however, has not been recognized as an ecological force in current policies of forest management in North America (Wisdom et al. 2006) (fig. 5). The magnitude of herbivory effects is neither recognized nor easily predicted under different combinations of episodic disturbance (fire, insect outbreaks), particularly across large landscapes (Weisburg and Bugman 2003). Therefore, the optimum sampling scheme for long-term vegetation change will include an exclosure design (Bakker and Moore 2007).

If both wild and domestic ungulates are present, then a three-way system for monitoring herbivory is required if their relative effects are to be assessed. Riggs et al. (2000) were able to differentiate between domestic and wild ungulate herbivory effects across a series of exclosures constructed in eastern Oregon in the 1960s. In western Colorado sagebrush steppe landscapes, Manier and Hobbs (2007) likewise were able to isolate long-term wild and domestic ungulate grazing effects upon plant community structure, biological diversity, and NPP.

In the West, experimental ranges are fortuitously situated to complement other national monitoring systems. The National Ecological Observatory Network (NEON) is a platform designed to monitor changes to U.S. ecosystems within 20 climatic domains over the next 30 years (Senkowsky 2005) (fig. 5). Western domains are not as well represented by dedicated

Figure 5.—*Secondary succession after stand replacement fire with and without (fenced area) ungulate herbivory influence. Photo credit: Travis Wall.*

NEON monitoring sites as those in the East (Keller et al. 2008), and most Forest Service and Agricultural Research Service experimental ranges are found in the West.

The location of a study area can limit the frequency of sampling. Johnson (2003) reported on a long-term study accessible only on horseback in the Eagle Cap Wilderness of northeastern Oregon. Plots were established by two different scientists at two different locations, one in 1907 and the other in 1938. The 1938 plots were reevaluated in 1953, 1959, and 1999 (table 1). The most significant change to composition occurred during the 1959 to 1999 timeframe, 20 to 60 years after plot establishment, thus illustrating the need for recurrent sampling to identify key periods of successional change. In another nearby location, Reid et al. (1991) concluded that the most significant plant community change occurred between the 30th and 40th years after plot establishment. Fortunately, difficult access is seldom an issue when sampling on EFRs.

What to sample and how often then become the drivers of sampling design. Plant community composition change is often the primary purpose in long-term data collection (Smith et al. 1986). Sampling often takes place at 5-year intervals. However, sampling should occur immediately after a disturbance such as fire, logging, or flooding in the case of riparian systems, and the 5-year sequence should be reset to the postdisturbance sampling timeframe. Although cover and frequency are acceptable parameters to sample and have been used for many years (Brown 1954, USDA Forest Service 1962), consideration must be given to both the type of vegetation and the ability of the individuals doing the sampling over time. Cover can be estimated using a number of different methods that employ plots, lines, and points. Cover has also been shown as an effective way to estimate aboveground plant biomass in arid communities (Flombaum and Sala 2007). Cover can be measured in two ways: (1) canopy cover and (2) basal cover. Both methods have advantages and disadvantages that vary with the ecosystem and the species being monitored.

Frequent measurements should be considered for precipitation and air and soil temperature. Monthly precipitation and maximum and minimum temperatures could be considered a minimum, and continuous recording temperature and precipitation devices the optimum. After 10 years of monitoring on the Santa Rita Experimental Range, Martin and Cable (1974)

concluded that the amount of rainfall, when it fell, and the duration of rainy and drought periods influenced the vegetation more strongly than did any other factor studied.

The development of long-term monitoring requires a commitment on the part of administrators for continued funding and on the part of scientists for continued sampling. These commitments must extend through personnel changes. This commitment is a real challenge because scientists may not reap immediate rewards for the effort.

Conclusions

The availability of EFRs, together with other national networks, provides an exciting opportunity for natural resource research. To successfully provide long-term biotic and abiotic data that can support broad-scale research into contemporary issues, such as climate change, species invasions, desertification, and fire, these EFRs must be connected in a network. A larger framework organized on connectivity provides more than an assemblage of data sets from different locations; it affords an opportunity to integrate information in a way that allows the kind of multidisciplinary research needed to address the complex problems now affecting our Nation's natural resources.

Literature Cited

Allen, T.F.H.; Hoekstra, T.W. 1992. Toward a unified ecology. New York: Columbia University Press. 384 p.

Angel, D.L.; McClaran, M.P. 2001. Long-term influences of livestock management and a non-native grass on grass dynamics on the desert grassland. Journal of Arid Environments. 49: 507–520.

Asner, G.P.; Elmore, A.J.; Olander, L.P., et al. 2004. Grazing systems, ecosystem responses, and global change. Annual Reviews in Environmental Research. 29: 261–299.

Augustine, D.J.; McNaughton, S.J. 1998. Ungulate effects on the functional species composition of plant communities: herbivore selectivity and plant tolerance. Journal of Wildland Management. 62: 1065–1083.

Bakker, J.D.; Moore, M.M. 2007. Controls on vegetation structure in southwestern ponderosa pine forests, 1941 and 2004. Ecology. 88: 2305–2319.

Bonham, C.D. 1989. Measurements for terrestrial vegetation. New York: John Wiley & Sons. 338 p.

Brown, D. 1954. Methods of surveying and measuring vegetation. Bull. 42. Commonwealth Bureau of Pasture and Field Crops. Hurley, Berkshire, England. 223 p.

Buffington, L.C.; Herbel, C.H. 1965. Vegetational changes on a semi-desert grassland range from 1858 to 1963. Ecological Monographs. 35: 139–164.

Costello, D.F.; Schwan, H.E. 1946. Conditions and trends on ponderosa pine ranges in Colorado. Unpublished report. Fort Collins, CO: U.S. Department of Agriculture, Forest Service, Rocky Mountain Forest and Range Experiment Station.

Crisp, D.; Johnson, C. 2005. The orbiting carbon observatory mission. Acta Astronautica. 56(1–2): 193–197.

Daily, G.C., ed. 1997. Nature's services: societal dependence on natural ecosystems. Washington, DC: Island Press. 392 p.

Flombaum, P.; Sala, O.A. 2007. A non-destructive and rapid method to estimate biomass and aboveground net primary production in arid environments. Journal of Arid Environments. 69: 352–358.

Follett, R.F. 2001. Organic carbon pools in grazing land soils. In: Follett, R.F.; Kimble, J.M.; Lal, R., eds. The potential of U.S. grazing lands to sequester carbon and mitigate the greenhouse effect. Boca Raton, FL: Lewis Publishers: 65–86.

Frayer, W.E.; Furnival, G.M. 1999. Forest survey sampling designs: a history. Journal of Forestry. 97(12): 4–10.

Gibbens, R.P.; Beck, R.F. 1988. Changes in grass basal area and forb densities over a 64-year period on grassland types of the Jornada Experimental Range. Journal of Range Management. 41: 186–192.

Hall, F.C. 2002. Photopoint monitoring handbook: part A—field procedures. Gen. Tech. Rep. PNW-GTR-526. Portland, OR: U.S. Department of Agriculture, Forest Service, Pacific Northwest Research Station. 48 p.

Herrick, J.E.; Van Zee, J.W.; Havstad, K., et al. 2005. Monitoring manual for grassland, shrubland and savanna ecosystems. Tucson, AZ: U.S. Department of Agriculture, Agricultural Research Service, Jornada Experimental Range. Vol. 1: Quick start. 36 p.

Hobbs, N.T. 1996. Modification of ecosystems by ungulates. Journal of Wildland Management. 60: 695–713.

Holechek, J.L.; Pieper, R.D.; Herbel, C.H. 1998. Range management principles and practices. 3rd ed. Upper Saddle River, NJ: Prentice-Hall. 560 p.

Humphrey, R.R. 1962. Range ecology. New York: The Ronald Ress Company. 234 p.

Johnson, C.G., Jr. 2003. Green fescue rangelands: changes over time in the Wallowa Mountains. Gen. Tech. Rep. PNW-GTR-569. Portland, OR: U.S. Department of Agriculture, Forest Service, Pacific Northwest Research Station. 41 p.

Johnson, W.M. 1953. Effect of grazing intensity upon vegetation and cattle gains on ponderosa pine-bunchgrass ranges of the Front Range of Colorado. Circular 929. Washington, DC: U.S. Department of Agriculture. 36 p.

Kasten, K.L. 1984. Tenure and merit pay as rewards for research, teaching, and service at a research university. Journal of Higher Education. 55: 500–514.

Keller, M.; Schimel, D.S.; Hargrove, W.W.; Hoffman, F.M. 2008. A continental strategy for the National Ecological Observatory Network. Frontiers in Ecology and the Environment. 6: 282–284.

Klade, R.J. 2006. Building a research legacy: the Intermountain Station, 1911–1997. Gen. Tech. Rep. RMRS-GTR-184. Fort Collins, CO: U.S. Department of Agriculture, Forest Service, Rocky Mountain Research Station. 259 p.

Klipple, G.E.; Costello, D.F. 1960. Vegetation and cattle responses to different intensities of grazing on short-grass ranges on the central Great Plains. Tech. Bull. No. 1216. Fort Collins, CO: U.S. Department of Agriculture, Forest Service, Rocky Mountain Forest and Range Experiment Station. 81 p.

Lenoir, J.; Gégout, J.C.; Marquet, P.A., et al. 2008. A significant upward shift in plant species optimum elevation during the 20th century. Science. 320: 1768–1771.

Lugo, A.E.; Swanson, F.J.; Gonzalez, O.M., et al. 2006. Long-term research at the USDA Forest Service's experimental forests and ranges. BioScience. 56: 39–48.

Manier, D.J.; Hobbs, N.T. 2007. Large herbivores in sagebrush steppe ecosystems: livestock and wild ungulates influence structure and function. Oecologia. 152: 739–750.

Martin, S.C.; Cable, D.R. 1974. Managing semidesert grass-shrub ranges: vegetation responses to precipitation, grazing, soil texture, and mesquite control. U.S. Department of Agriculture Tech. Bull. 1480. Washington, DC: U.S. Department of Agriculture. 45 p.

Miles, J. 1979. Vegetation dynamics. London, United Kingdom: Chapman and Hall. 76 p.

Millennium Ecosystem Assessment. 2005. Ecosystems and human well-being: synthesis. Washington, DC: Island Press. 65 p.

Miller-Rushing, A.J.; Primack, R.B. 2008. Global warming and flowering times in Thoreau's Concord: a community perspective. Ecology. 89: 332–341.

Mitchell, J.E. 2000. Rangeland resource trends in the United States: a technical document supporting the 2000 USDA Forest Service RPA assessment. Gen. Tech. Rep. RMRS-GTR-68. Fort Collins, CO: U.S. Department of Agriculture, Forest Service, Rocky Mountain Research Station. 84 p.

Morgan, J.A.; Mosier, A.R.; Milchunas, D.G., et al. 2004. CO_2 enhances productivity, alters species composition, and reduces digestibility of shortgrass steppe vegetation. Ecological Applications. 14: 208–219.

Mueggler, W.F. 1992. Cliff Lake Bench Research Natural Area: problems encountered in monitoring vegetation change on grasslands. Res. Pap. INT-454. Ogden, UT: U.S. Department of Agriculture, Forest Service, Intermountain Research Station. 13 p.

Negra, C.; Sweedo, C.C.; Cavender-Bares, K., et al. 2008. Indicators of carbon storage in US ecosystems: baseline for terrestrial carbon. Journal of Environmental Quality. 37: 1376–1382.

Nusser, S.M.; Goebel, J.J. 1997. The National Resources Inventory: a long-term multi-resource monitoring programme. Environmental and Ecological Statistics. 4: 181–204.

Oakes, R. 2008. Personal communication. Site manager, U.S. Department of Agriculture, Forest Service, Rocky Mountain Research Station, Manitou Experimental Forest, Woodland Park, CO.

Owensby, C.E.; Ham, J.M.; Knapp, A.K.; Auen, L.M. 1999. Biomass production and species composition change in a tallgrass prairie ecosystem after long-term exposure to elevated atmospheric CO_2. Global Change Biology. 5: 497–506.

Pearson, H.A.; Clary, W.P.; Moore, M.M.; Sieg, C.H. 2008. Range management research, Fort Valley Experimental Forest. In: Olberding, S.D.; Moore, M.M., tech. coords. Fort Valley Experimental Forest—a century of research, 1908–2008. Proceedings RMRS-P-53CD. Fort Collins, CO: U.S. Department of Agriculture, Forest Service, Rocky Mountain Research Station. 408 p.

Pellant, M.; Shaver, P.; Pyke, D.A.; Herrick, J.E. 2000. Interpreting indicators of rangeland health. Tech. Ref. 1734-6. Washington, DC: U.S. Department of the Interior, Bureau of Land Management, Washington Office. 118 p.

Post, E.S.; Pedersen, C.; Wilmers, C.C.; Forchhammer, M.C. 2008. Phenological sequences reveal aggregate life history response to climatic warming. Ecology. 89: 363–370.

Powledge, F. 2008. Climate change and public lands. BioScience. 58: 912–918.

Pyke, D.A.; Herrick, J.E.; Shaver, P.; Pellant, M. 2002. Rangeland health attributes and indicators for qualitative assessment. Journal of Range Management. 55: 584–597.

Reid, E.H.; Johnson, C.G., Jr.; Hall, W.B. 1991. Green fescue grassland: 50 years of secondary succession under sheep grazing. R6-F16-SO-0591. Portland, OR: U.S. Department of Agriculture, Forest Service, Pacific Northwest Region, Wallowa-Whitman National Forest. 37 p.

Riggs, R.A.; Tiedemann, A.R.; Cook, J.G., et al. 2000. Modification of mixed-conifer forests by ruminant herbivores in the Blue Mountains ecological province. Res. Pap. PNW-RP-527. Portland, OR: U.S. Department of Agriculture, Forest Service, Pacific Northwest Research Station. 77 p.

Senkowsky, S. 2005. Planning of NEON moves ahead. BioScience. 55: 106–112.

Sharp, L.A.; Sanders, K.; Rimbey, N. 1990. Forty years of change in a shadscale stand in Idaho. Rangelands. 12: 313–328.

Skovlin, J.M.; Harris, R.W.; Strickler, G.S.; Garrison, G.A. 1976. Effects of cattle grazing methods on ponderosa pine-bunchgrass range in the Pacific Northwest. Tech. Bull. 1531. Portland, OR: U.S. Department of Agriculture, Forest Service, Pacific Northwest Research Station. 40 p.

Skovlin, J.M.; Thomas, J.W. 1995. Interpreting long-term trends in Blue Mountain ecosystems from repeat photography. Res. Pap. PNW GTR-315. Portland, OR: U.S. Department of Agriculture, Forest Service, Pacific Northwest Research Station. 102 p.

Smith, S.D.; Bunting, S.C.; Hironaka, M.1986. Sensitivity of frequency plots for detecting vegetation change. Northwest Science. 60: 279–286.

Swetnam, T.W.; Allen, C.D.; Betancourt, J.L. 1999. Applied historical ecology: using the past to manage for the future. Ecological Applications. 9: 1189–1206.

Talbert, C.; Knight, R.L.; Mitchell, J. 2007. Private ranch lands and public-land grazing in the southern Rocky Mountains. Rangelands. 29: 5–8.

U.S. Department of Agriculture (USDA) Forest Service. 1962. Range research methods. Misc. Publ. No. 940. Washington, DC: U.S. Department of Agriculture, Forest Service. 172 p.

Weisburg, P.J.; Bugman, H. 2003. Forest dynamics and ungulate herbivory: from leaf to landscape. Forest Ecology and Management. 18: 1–2.

Wisdom, M.J.; Vavra, M.; Boyd, J.M., et al. 2006. Understanding ungulate herbivory-episodic disturbance effects on vegetation dynamics: knowledge gaps and management needs. Wildlife Society Bulletin. 34: 283–292.

Using Existing Long-Term Thinning Studies To Investigate the Carbon Consequences of Thinning: Learning From the Past To Craft the Future

Coeli Hoover[1]

Abstract

Although long-term research is a critical tool for answering forest management questions, managers must often make decisions before results from such experiments are available. One way to meet those information needs is to reanalyze existing long-term data sets to address current research questions; the Forest Service Experimental Forests and Ranges (EFRs) network provides a plethora of opportunities for investigations of this nature. This study is a pilot test to assess the feasibility of using existing long-term data sets from density management studies to develop carbon sequestration estimates for forests across the United States; the objective is to generalize carbon implications of different thinning methods within and across geographic regions and forest types. Although long-term records from historic studies provide many opportunities, using these data presents many challenges, including lack of documentation and experimental design constraints. In this preliminary study, such obstacles did not permit the development of generalizations about the carbon consequences of density management treatments, although carbon stock estimates were developed for four different studies. In addition to carbon data, a discussion of the challenges inherent in working with existing long-term records is presented, as well as specific recommendations to facilitate the use of long-term experiments for retrospective and/or synthetic analyses.

Introduction

Many forestry and ecology research questions require, by their nature, a long-term research approach. This observation is especially true in forestry, where rotation lengths are often many decades long and the lifespan of individual trees may be measured in centuries. Many investigators have made compelling arguments for the need for large-scale, carefully designed, long-term research studies (Franklin et al. 1990, Powers 1999, Powers et al. 1994); a primary reason given is that short-term and long-term responses can differ (e.g., Sanchez et al. 2006, Scott et al. 2004, Zhang et al. 2005). Such long-term studies may not offer initial results until 5 to 10 years after installation, with the main results often not available for decades. Meanwhile, managers need guidelines on a much shorter timeframe. One solution to meeting these needs is to use retrospective studies, in which the researcher takes advantage of past treatments or events. Conducting a retrospective study may include remeasuring plots established for a previous study, analyzing existing long-term data, or both. The Forest Service network of EFRs (Adams et al. 2008, Lugo et al. 2006) features many preexisting long-term studies, which provide ample opportunity to seek answers to contemporary problems in a variety of forest types. There are numerous uses for existing long-term data, such as investigating the possible impacts of climate change, tracking changes in phenology and species composition, seeking patterns or changes in insect and disease outbreaks, and assessing the carbon implications of management practices.

Powers (1989) provides an excellent overview of the challenges and opportunities presented by retrospective studies. Of particular note is the list of eight critical questions to ask when planning a study. These questions address adequate replication, identification of confounding factors, and other elements of experimental design. Many, although not all, challenges encountered in this study are related to points raised by Powers (1989, 1994). Although constraints exist, the potential importance of retrospective studies is evidenced by the database of baseline information for more than 170 sites in Washington and Oregon assembled by Thomas et al. (1993) for the specific

---

[1] Ecologist, U S Department of Agriculture Forest Service, Northern Research Station, Durham, NH

purpose of facilitating such studies. In addition to retrospective studies addressing questions that are quite different from the purpose of the original experiment, in many cases an ongoing study benefits greatly from remeasuring a study intended for a short-term purpose that was completed in the past. If the original plots can be relocated and the measurement protocols are well documented, then the opportunity exists to convert a completed short-term experiment into a long-term, and more useful, investigation. Examples of this type of work include Dolph et al. (1995) and Pitt and Lanteigne (2008).

This investigation was undertaken as an extension of a retrospective analysis of data from a long-term thinning study on the Kane Experimental Forest in northwestern Pennsylvania. Data from an experiment that was established in 1975 to examine the effects of different thinning approaches on the growth and yield of an Allegheny hardwood stand were used to assess the effects of the thinning treatments on carbon sequestration (Hoover and Stout 2007). The original intent of this current study was a set of baseline carbon sequestration estimates for various major forest types across the United States, to generalize carbon implications of different thinning methods within and across geographic regions. The focus is on carbon in aboveground live tree biomass only. Due to the challenges and constraints discussed in the following text, however, the goal of this study became an investigation into the feasibility of applying the approach of Hoover and Stout (2007) to other existing long-term data sets from areas described in Adams et al. (2008). The objectives included (1) assembling a sufficient number of data sets to have examples from several forest types, (2) presenting preliminary carbon sequestration results from four long-term thinning data sets, and (3) evaluating the use of this collection of experimental data sets and providing a series of recommendations to facilitate retrospective and/or synthetic analysis now and in the future. This paper is not intended as an indepth analysis of carbon sequestration at these few sites but rather as a trail map for maximizing the usefulness of priceless data from long-term studies.

Methods

An informal survey was developed and sent to all members of the Forest Service EFRs mailing list, which reaches the designated point of contact for all sites listed in Adams et al.

(2008). The survey asked a variety of questions regarding the existence of long-term inventory records, the presence of active and closed thinning studies, the nature of the inventory design, and the state and format of the study records. Possible candidates for analysis were chosen from the replies, and requests were sent for the inventory records and any supporting materials such as study plans and establishment reports.

Because the inventory records are from different regions, the generalized biomass equations of Jenkins et al. (2003) were used to produce biomass estimates. These equations do not require height as an input variable. The minimum data required for this study are species, diameter at breast height (d.b.h.), tree status (live, dead, cut, ingrowth), thinning treatment applied, and plot size. Although many of the study designs included individually numbered stems, some tallies took the form of number of trees by species and diameter class. Either type of data can be used for biomass estimates using the generalized equations, although the individual stem records provide more precise information. The resulting biomass estimates were multiplied by 0.5 to convert to carbon. Results were summarized by experimental forest, by treatment, and average annual net carbon change was calculated and presented.

One forest included treatments that involved extensive harvesting, in which a notable amount of carbon was transferred into harvested wood products. A retrospective analysis of carbon in harvested wood products is possible in cases in which detailed harvest records were kept. Accounting for carbon in harvested wood products is a complex topic; I followed the methods described in Smith et al. (2006). To simplify the accounting, slash was not included in the estimates because detailed carbon budgets are not the focus of these case studies.

Results and Discussion

Carbon Sequestration

Of the 27 surveys received, I was able to successfully use data from four experimental forests to estimate forest carbon storage over time. The sites are the Bartlett Experimental Forest (northern hardwoods), Vinton Furnace Experimental Forest (mixed oak), Crossett Experimental Forest (loblolly/shortleaf pine), and Wind River Experimental Forest (Douglas-fir). All four forests are located in the conterminous United States; figure 1 shows the approximate location of each site. Adams et al. (2008) supplies further details on these and other sites in the Forest Service EFRs network. Issues with data that were not used are presented and discussed in the next section.

Bartlett Experimental Forest, New Hampshire—Thinning Young, Even-Aged Northern Hardwoods

This experiment was installed in 1959 in a 25-year-old, even-aged northern hardwood stand. Four thinning treatments were applied: heavy crop tree, light crop tree, weeding, and no thinning (control); each treatment was replicated five times. All stems 5 cm d.b h. and above were tallied at each inventory. Details of the study design and early results were described by Marquis (1969). In 1972, the study was amended to add additional release and fertilization of crop trees on the plots assigned to the weeding treatment. Because of the change in treatments, data from the weeding plots were excluded from the carbon analysis. The study continues today; the plots were

retreated in 2003 and the treatments were altered at that time to address slightly different questions.

Carbon stock estimates for aboveground live tree biomass in the precommercial thinning study on the Bartlett Experimental Forest are given in table 1. At the time of the last measurement, standing carbon stocks in live biomass ranged from about 80 metric tons/hectare (t C/ha) in the heavily thinned plots to about 95 t C/ha in the unthinned plots. Mean carbon increment (average annual change) for the entire analysis period differed slightly, from 1.2 t C/ha/yr in heavily thinned plots to 1.5 t C/ha/yr in unthinned control plots. Because not all data sets include pretreatment data, mean carbon increment is calculated for the entire study duration and from the first posttreatment measurement until about 15 years after treatment for each study. In the Bartlett study, mean carbon increment from 1964 through 1975 was 2.6 t C/ha in the heavily thinned plots and 1.6 t C/ha in the control plots; lightly thinned plots stored 2.4 t C/ha/yr for that period.

Figure 1.—*Approximate location of study sites.*

Vinton Furnace Experimental Forest, Ohio—Mixed Oak Stocking Study

This stocking study was initiated in 1962 in stands that were 55 to 65 years old at the time of study establishment. Six density levels were used: 40, 50, 60, 70, 80, and 100 percent of full stocking. Treatments were replicated, although each density level did not have the same number of replicates. The 80-percent level was applied to a single plot and so was excluded from the carbon analysis. The study establishment report provides details on the installation procedures as well as results from the first remeasurement and includes observations on measurement discrepancies, growing season drought, and heavy mortality in two plots. Although the report describes a pretreatment tally, these data were not available and the carbon stock estimates begin with posttreatment inventories. This situation is not uncommon; pretreatment inventories were often dot tallies of the number of stems by species and diameter class, with individual stem numbering begun after the first treatment. When data are transferred from paper to electronic formats, the initial dot tally is sometimes not included. The minimum d.b h. for tally is 3.8 cm.

Live aboveground carbon stocks in the mixed oak stocking study are given in table 2 for four density levels and the unthinned control. Although most treatments are represented by four plots, the 70-percent density level has only two plots, and there is a single unthinned plot. Average aboveground live tree carbon stocks were similar across density levels in 2006, ranging from a maximum of 107 t C/ha in the control plot to a low of 96 t C/ha for the 50-percent density treatment. Over the entire study, the highest mean carbon increment of 1.4 t C/ha/yr occurs in the 40-percent treatment, with the lowest rates in the 70-percent density treatment (0.9 t C/ha/yr) and the control plot (0.7 t C/ha/yr). During the period from 1962 through 1976, mean carbon increment was similar in the 40-, 50-, and 60-percent treatments (1.5 to 1.7 t C/ha) and lowest in the control plot, which stored 0.1 t C/ha/yr over that period.

Table 1.—Carbon stock in live aboveground biomass (tonnes C/ha) for the Bartlett Experimental Forest precommercial thinning trial.[a] Standard error of the mean is given in parentheses.

Measurement year	Heavy	Light	Control
1958[b]	41.2 (1.49)	46.6 (2.05)	48.2 (3.48)
1964	40.2 (1.65)	50.2 (2.01)	61.2 (2.00)
1969	56.0 (2.39)	65.0 (3.13)	69.7 (2.22)
1975	69.4 (1.78)	76.7 (1.44)	78.5 (0.66)
1990	79.9 (0.52)	88.3 (4.24)	94.8 (5.22)
Mean C increment[c] 1964–75	2.6 (0.17)	2.4 (0.07)	1.6 (0.20)
Mean C increment 1958–90	1.2 (0.15)	1.3 (0.10)	1.5 (0.22)

C = carbon. ha = hectare.

[a] See text for study description.

[b] Data from 1958 are pretreatment; 1964 is the first posttreatment measurement year.

[c] Mean C increment is average annual change (t C/ha/yr) over the time interval.

Table 2.—Carbon stock in live aboveground biomass (tonnes C/ha) for the Vinton Furnace Experimental Forest oak stocking study.[a] Standard error of the mean is given in parentheses.

Measurement year	40%	50%	60%	70%	100%
1962[b]	38.0 (1.47)	43.8 (1.30)	51.0 (1.13)	61.9 (2.40)	75.7 (NA)
1966	40.5 (0.80)	47.3 (0.53)	55.0 (1.43)	62.4 (1.43)	76.2 (NA)
1976	58.9 (3.81)	68.0 (1.90)	71.4 (1.35)	72.7 (0.96)	77.4 (NA)
1984	72.8 (6.15)	81.6 (3.54)	85.2 (1.72)	83.6 (0.64)	90.3 (NA)
1996	83.0 (7.74)	86.4 (4.84)	88.4 (3.30)	90.1 (4.78)	91.7 (NA)
2006	98.2 (7.21)	95.9 (3.47)	99.6 (4.40)	101.0 (5.82)	107.4 (NA)
Mean C increment[c] 1962–76	1.5 (0.20)	1.7 (0.09)	1.5 (0.13)	0.8 (0.24)	0.1 (NA)
Mean C increment 1962–2006	1.4 (0.16)	1.2 (0.07)	1.1 (0.12)	0.9 (0.08)	0.7 (NA)

C = carbon. ha = hectare. NA = no data available.

[a] See text for study description.

[b] Data from 1962 are posttreatment.

[c] Mean C increment is average annual change (t C/ha/yr) over the time interval.

Crossett Experimental Forest, Arkansas—Methods of Cut Study in Natural Loblolly/Shortleaf Pine

This method of cut study began in 1943, and the following treatments were applied: merchantable clearcut, diameter limit cut, heavy seed tree cut, and selection cutting. Followup treatments were applied as scheduled according to the study design (multiple retreatments occurred), with the clearcut and seed tree cuts thinned from below, the diameter limit cut repeated, and the selection cut was managed on 5-year cutting cycles to maintain a specified volume. Each treatment was replicated three times and hardwood competition was controlled through various methods throughout the study. All pine stems 10 cm d.b h. and above were tallied. A few instances of windthrow during the course of the study were severe enough to warrant salvage, but detailed records were not kept on the salvage operation. For this analysis, this circumstance was addressed by ending the carbon analysis in 1990, the measurement before extensive windthrow damage. Although the decision was made to stop measurements in 1957 on the clearcut plots because principal investigators had determined that those plots were successfully regenerated, measurements and thinning treatments were resumed on these plots in 1979 (Cain and Shelton 2001). This study had a notable amount of carbon transferred into the harvested wood products pool, as compared to the amount of forest carbon. For this reason, two sets of results will be presented: carbon in live aboveground biomass and carbon in live aboveground biomass plus carbon in harvested wood products.

Carbon stock estimates are given in tables 3 and 4 for the methods of cut study. Table 3 is similar to previous tables and

Table 3.—*Carbon stock in live aboveground biomass (tonnes C/ha) for the Crossett Experimental Forest methods of cut study.*[a] *Standard error of the mean is given in parentheses.*

Measurement year	Commercial clearcut	Diameter limit	Seed tree	Selection cut
1942[b]	30.7 (4.78)	27.6 (0.52)	30.3 (2.98)	33.1 (2.93)
1947	0.9 (0.25)	14.2 (0.25)	12.2 (0.71)	31.8 (1.14)
1952	8.2 (1.31)	22.8 (19.2)	20.0 (1.23)	37.4 (0.30)
1957	27.5 (3.27)	19.2 (2.30)	33.0 (1.65)	39.4 (1.92)
1962	NA	26.5 (0.96)	17.0 (0.25)	36.5 (0.61)
1967	NA	42.6 (2.31)	33.9 (2.38)	41.5 (1.88)
1979	62.7 (2.01)	39.5 (0.96)	63.8 (2.88)	50.8 (2.99)
1985	56.0 (1.72)	11.9 (0.53)	55.0 (0.99)	37.1 (3.16)
1990	54.0 (2.05)	17.3 (1.05)	53.8 (0.89)	36.7 (1.80)
Mean C increment[c] 1942–57	− 0.2 (0.44)	− 0.6 (0.02)	0.2 (0.29)	0.4 (0.29)
Mean C increment 1942–90	0.5 (0.07)	− 0.2 (0.02)	0.5 (0.07)	0.1 (0.06)

C = carbon. ha = hectare. NA = no data available.

[a] *See text for study description.*

[b] *Data from 1942 are pretreatment; 1947 is the first posttreatment measurement year.*

[c] *Mean C increment is average annual change (t C/ha/yr) over the time interval.*

Table 4.—*Carbon stock in live aboveground biomass and harvested wood (tonnes C/ha) for the Crossett Experimental Forest methods of cut study.*[a] *Standard error of the mean is given in parentheses.*

Measurement year	Commercial clearcut	Diameter limit	Seed tree	Selection cut
1942[b]	30.7 (4.78)	27.6 (0.52)	30.3 (2.98)	33.1 (2.93)
1947	11.4 (1.63)	20.5 (0.32)	18.9 (0.56)	34.3 (1.49)
1952	17.7 (1.42)	28.6 (0.20)	25.8 (0.80)	41.0 (0.76)
1957	36.3 (3.03)	29.0 (1.62)	38.3 (0.92)	45.4 (1.05)
1962	NA	37.9 (2.54)	31.1 (0.18)	45.6 (0.94)
1967	NA	53.4 (1.93)	47.0 (2.18)	51.9 (2.10)
1979	70.2 (3.28)	57.9 (0.72)	75.9 (2.65)	63.6 (3.20)
1985	70.9 (1.95)	40.8 (0.20)	73.6 (1.06)	55.8 (4.18)
1990	71.6 (3.51)	44.3 (0.93)	74.5 (1.32)	56.4 (3.56)
Mean C increment[c] 1942–57	0.4 (0.34)	0.1 (0.14)	0.5 (0.24)	0.8 (0.24)
Mean C increment 1942–90	0.9 (0.04)	0.3 (0.01)	0.9 (0.08)	0.5 (0.08)

C = carbon. ha = hectare. NA = no data available.

[a] *See text for study description.*

[b] *Data from 1942 are pretreatment; 1947 is the first posttreatment measurement year.*

[c] *Mean C increment is average annual change (t C/ha/yr) over the time interval.*

reports the carbon stock estimates for aboveground live tree biomass. Table 4 provides estimates for carbon in aboveground live tree biomass plus carbon in harvested wood products. Table 4 is presented to demonstrate that such accounting is possible in a retrospective analysis. Note that although the values for each treatment are different in tables 3 and 4, the overall outcomes are the same. Mean carbon increment over the entire study period was lowest in the diameter limit treatment and highest in the seed tree and commercial clearcuts with and without the inclusion of harvested wood products. Similarly, for the 1942 through 1957 period, mean carbon increment was highest in the selection cut and lowest in the diameter limit treatment, regardless of products. Live aboveground biomass carbon stocks in 1991 ranged from about 54 t C/ha in the commercial clearcut and seed tree treatments to 17 t C/ha in the diameter limit plots; the selection cut averaged 37 t C/ha.

Wind River Experimental Forest, Oregon—Douglas-Fir Spacing Test

This spacing test was initiated in 1925 by planting seedlings at square spacings of 1.2, 1.5, 1.8, 2.4, 3, and 3.67 m (4, 5, 6, 8, 10, and 12 ft). True replicates were not used; each spacing was applied to a single block, and measurements were taken on subplots within each block (generally three plots, although four were used in the 2.4-m spacing, and two plots were sampled in the 3.67-m spacing). In the first few years after establishment, heavy seedling mortality required the replanting of many seedlings. When the measurement plots were laid out in 1945, investigators noticed that not all plots in a block had similar soil characteristics and adjustments were made to address this observation. The 3.67-m spacing was installed on a smaller block and sampled on two small subplots; for this reason, data from this treatment were not used for the carbon analysis. Tree measurements were generally made every 5 years (stems 3.8 cm d.b.h. and above), and soil studies were begun in the 1970s. Investigators learned that soils at the southern end of the site are deeper and have greater available water-holding capacity. Although the spacing test was laid out in blocks, each block represents a single spacing treatment; treatments were not randomized within blocks. The blocks with the closest spacing are located at the northern end of the site; soil properties and spacing treatments are confounded. After careful study of the growth and soils data, however, Miller et al. (2004) concluded that, although soil properties are a factor in the growth results, tree spacing likely plays a stronger role. This careful documentation and followup work allows us to learn from the Wind River study even though design problems exist.

In the Wind River study, large differences are apparent in the live aboveground biomass carbon stocks at the last measurement (table 5). As noted previously, site differences are confounded with the spacing treatments; however, the study still provides valuable estimates of carbon stock change under different conditions. In 1991, carbon stocks were similar in the 1.5-, 1.8-, and 2.4-m spacings, ranging from 104 to 112 t C/ha; however, the average carbon stock in the 3-m (10-ft) spacing treatment was nearly double that in the 1.2-m spacing. Although this result is likely due to a combination of spacing

Table 5.—*Carbon stock in live aboveground biomass (tonnes C/ha) for the Wind River Experimental Forest spacing study.[a] Standard error of the mean is given in parentheses.*

Measurement year	1.2 x 1.2 m	1.5 x 1.5 m	1.8 x 1.8 m	2.4 x 2.4 m	3 x 3 m
1945[b]	38.2 (2.84)	29.4 (2.47)	27.8 (1.39)	23.4 (6.94)	24.5 (2.53)
1951	58.5 (4.67)	48.2 (3.22)	48.0 (2.13)	35.0 (3.35)	51.7 (5.05)
1957	72.2 (6.44)	62.8 (3.88)	64.1 (3.00)	58.2 (3.92)	75.5 (7.86)
1960	81.1 (7.61)	70.3 (4.30)	73.0 (4.50)	70.2 (4.58)	91.3 (8.02)
1965	81.7 (4.32)	76.3 (4.50)	77.3 (5.69)	80.4 (4.68)	105.3 (8.56)
1970	80.9 (1.90)	82.4 (5.65)	83.0 (7.40)	86.2 (4.88)	122.2 (9.32)
1975	83.1 (1.68)	88.1 (5.92)	87.8 (9.27)	93.7 (5.25)	135.8 (9.38)
1980	89.0 (1.73)	95.0 (6.27)	95.6 (11.87)	101.9 (6.26)	150.7 (8.34)
1986	92.7 (1.62)	101.9 (6.99)	102.0 (13.12)	109.3 (6.33)	163.5 (7.89)
1991	92.8 (3.46)	104.6 (6.44)	104.2 (15.68)	111.9 (6.07)	175.1 (7.79)
Mean C increment[c] 1945–60	2.9 (0.32)	2.7 (0.12)	3.0 (0.27)	3.1 (0.30)	4.5 (0.37)
Mean C increment 1945–91	1.2 (0.10)	1.6 (0.09)	1.7 (0.33)	1.9 (0.06)	3.3 (0.12)

C = carbon. ha = hectare.

[a] See text for study description.

[b] Data from 1945 are posttreatment.

[c] Mean C increment is average annual change (t C/ha/yr) over the time interval.

effects and moisture availability, it demonstrates the large range of carbon storage potential possible. Mean carbon increment over the entire measurement period ranged from 1.2 t C/ha/yr in the 1.2-m spacing to 1.9 t C/ha/yr in the 2.4-m treatment. Again, the 3-m spacing had a much higher mean carbon increment, storing 3.3 t C/ha/yr. Mean carbon increment for the 1945 through 1960 interval followed a similar pattern, ranging from 2.9 to 3.1 t C/ha/yr except in the 3-m treatment, which stored an average of 4.5 t C/ha/yr in that time period.

Generalizations From the Case Studies

Although there are difficulties to overcome, analysis of existing data from density management studies is a feasible way to investigate the effects of varied treatments on forest carbon storage (although considerable time is required to collect, clean, and collate records). For situations in which control plot data exist, baseline carbon accumulation estimates for various forest types can also be developed, as well as estimates of biomass in standing dead trees and the impacts of insect and disease outbreaks (in cases in which detailed mortality codes were employed). These initial results highlight the contrast between short-term and long-term results; managers wishing to consider carbon sequestration as one of several management goals need to consider whether net carbon storage or the rate of carbon uptake is the variable of concern, and over what timeframe. Of the four cases presented here, two are thinning studies (Bartlett and Vinton Furnace). In both cases, the average annual rate of carbon storage over the short term was higher in the thinned plots; long-term rates were also higher for thinned plots at Vinton Furnace (and similar among treatments at Bartlett). This observation suggests that the approach of using long-term data sets to develop generalizations about the carbon implications of management treatments is valid and that the analysis will bear fruit. In addition, these studies highlight factors worth considering when developing management strategies for carbon sequestration, such as the importance of site characteristics (Wind River) and regeneration methods (Crossett).

Challenges in Using These Data

There is a set of common problems that arise when using long-term data sets. Many of these problems have been described in detail; e.g., Burger and Powers (1991) and Curtis and Marshall

(2005). Most can be avoided only during the planning stage of the experiment, although careful attention to documenting and maintaining records is necessary throughout the life of the study. Careful recordkeeping may allow a useful analysis to be conducted even if design shortcomings exist. Inadequate recordkeeping, however, can render even the most soundly designed experiment unusable to future investigators.

Challenges encountered in the course of this pilot study included many of those commonly encountered by others. The most significant challenges included the following:

- Lack of knowledge of existing data sets—the "file drawer syndrome." The survey questionnaire asked for negative and positive replies. Although some respondents indicated that the forest in question had no current or past long-term studies, a common reply was that the individual listed as the point of contact was unsure of what data existed or of the current condition or location of records. As studies are completed and closed, personnel retire or transfer, and offices move or consolidate, data files and associated documents may change hands many times. In meta-analysis, the "file drawer problem" refers to the risk of analyses that are compromised by the small number of published reports of statistically nonsignificant results. In long-term studies, there is, quite literally, a file drawer problem. Investigators and project managers inherit file cabinets full of records from closed studies; these records can provide valuable opportunities for retrospective studies and synthesis activities. In many cases, however, those records have not been cataloged and site personnel may have little idea of the contents of those file cabinets. Cataloging and documenting records requires large amounts of time, but the investment can provide large returns.

- Lack of replication. Experimental designs did not always include replication for all treatments. Early studies often incorporated multiple levels and/or combinations of intermediate treatments, sometimes resulting in just one or two plots representing a specific treatment. This scenario makes it quite difficult to draw any generalizations about the response of a stand to a particular treatment, limiting the usefulness of the retrospective approach. Since long-term studies are especially vulnerable to losses from disturbance, inadequate replication presents a significant challenge for investigators planning retrospective studies or synthesis activities.

- Absence of control plots and/or pretreatment data. Sites in the Forest Service network of EFRs have been the setting for experimental research since the 1930s. Many records exist from studies that were installed from the 1930s through the 1950s, and these studies are particularly valuable for their length of record. When these earlier studies were installed, however, experimental design and research approaches had a different focus from contemporary approaches. In many cases, the level of treatment was of interest, not the performance of treated versus untreated stands, so control plots were not installed. In addition, if the method of cutting or level of cutting was the area of interest, stand growth after harvest was the important variable and pretreatment measurements were often not taken. Resources are almost always scarce and larger scale experiments have high costs, so the decisions not to install untreated controls or take pretreatment data were made. Unfortunately, those same decisions limit the usefulness of experiments to supply baseline data or provide answers to the questions of today and tomorrow.

- Inconsistency/inadequacy of documentation. This issue is an ongoing challenge in any long-term research project. Technology, personnel, methods, study objectives, and record formats are just a few of the items that can change over time. In the case of the current study, tree status codes were a particular problem; codes were often unexplained or inconsistent with the data file, resulting in stems coded as dead that continued to increase in diameter as well as live trees with static diameter measurements. The reuse of a tree number from a dead or cut tree created difficulties in a few cases and is a common problem in long-term forestry studies. Coding of diameters also changed over time in at least one data set, with records for some years containing an implied decimal point while in other years the decimal point was explicitly recorded. In some cases, treatments were changed to address questions that had arisen since the study was installed. Although alterations of treatments were generally well documented, growth records from these plots could not be used for carbon analysis due to the change in treatment. Disturbance events also occurred; in some studies this situation was fairly well documented while in other studies only general notes were provided, making it difficult to discern the extent and impact of the disturbance on the response variables.

Lessons Learned

Although the original goals of this project were not met, this pilot test demonstrates that it is feasible to use long-term data sets from thinning trials to develop carbon estimates, although substantial time and effort are currently required to locate, acquire, clean, and understand the data files for use. Although the stated objective of this study was to glean insight into the carbon consequences of thinning treatments, the primary lessons learned are about the design and maintenance of long-term studies. Careful design can position an experiment to be useful well into the future and for purposes other than originally intended. Inadequate design and planning can greatly limit the usefulness of a study for future efforts, and the failure to properly document, maintain, and catalog records can doom even the most robustly designed experiment.

The key lessons learned in this pilot test are primarily related to documentation:

- *Working with older data sets is like solving a puzzle.* Many cases of insufficient documentation result because an investigator plans a study and expects to complete the study during his or her career. Often, this situation is exactly what occurs. The results are published, and the scientist moves on to the next project, not anticipating that another investigator may wish to reopen the study in the future or use the data for retrospective analysis or meta-analysis. Often, the required documentation exists but may be located in several different places and in different formats.

- *Nothing is obvious.* Is diameter measured in inches? What are the units for plot size? What measure of relative density is being used? Were board feet calculated using Doyle? Failure to document the obvious can require that others conduct a great deal of detective work. In some cases, this situation can render data unusable for any future analyses. Although data sets may have been transferred from paper tally sheets to electronic files, units and other key information are not always included.

- *Formats change.* Electronic data are extremely useful and can save a great deal of time. Data formats change rapidly, however, and money and staff time are not always available to update files to current formats. For example, Marshall and Deitschman (1976) describe a computer program written to facilitate the use of existing long-term data. They note the importance of backing up the data and keeping a copy off site. The method chosen for data storage was tape; of course, such tapes cannot be read today. Marshall and Deitschman (1976) also report that original tally sheets and printouts of the master data files were maintained on site. Regrettably, electronic files do not render paper records unnecessary.

- *Recollections are not always accurate.* Many investigators inherit studies and data sets and may not be familiar with the state of the records. Before planning a study involving particular data sets, it is helpful to examine a subset of the actual data records. Data sets may not always be "as advertised."

- Although retrospective analysis is a short cut, it still requires considerable time to locate data records and supporting documentation and to clean, understand, and update the files. *These tasks can often take more time than conducting the actual analysis.*

Recommendations and Conclusions

The following is a list of major recommendations to consider when planning, installing, and implementing experimental studies. These recommendations are intended to facilitate the use of a study for future analyses addressing issues that are currently unknown, as well as cross-site synthesis activities.

- Document the obvious; do not make assumptions. Especially as meta-analysis becomes more commonly used, it is better to provide too much detail than too little. Be sure to provide details on measurement units, plot sizes, treatment codes, mortality codes, species codes, measures of density, size cutoffs, disturbance events, etc. When in doubt, include the information.

- Keep key metadata in the main data file with the measurement. Although supplementary files such as study plans, establishment reports, and interim results are extremely useful, they can easily become separated from the main data files over time. The key metadata (see point mentioned previously) should be included in the main data file. For example, if using a spreadsheet, the first page in the workbook should include the critical metadata. Do not rely on documentation in additional files.

- Check records and formats for consistency over time. If species codes or mortality codes were changed or treatments

were altered, the data records should be updated to reflect this change, or the changes must be documented in the metadata. Failure to document such changes can easily render a data set unusable. Records should be checked each time that new data are entered to detect problems such as incorrect mortality codes, reuse of tree numbers, tree diameters getting smaller, etc. Such discrepancies are much easier to clear up shortly after measurement than decades in the future.

- Think long term when considering record storage. Consider keeping paper copies of records in case formats are not updated in a timely manner.

- Apply the "bus test" to every data set for which you are responsible. If you were hit by a speeding bus tomorrow, would a colleague who is only slightly familiar with your study be able to understand and use your data? If the answer is yes, then your study is adequately documented and can be useful well into the future. If not, then add the critical metadata to the data files.

- Take time to tend data sets. If you inherit a long-term data set from another investigator, take the time to become familiar with it. Addressing any documentation problems at the time of transfer is much simpler than it will be a decade or two in the future. Be sure to update documentation as needed; in many cases, a disturbance event can provide opportunities for new studies if adequate documentation is available. In addition, data may still be usable, even if a disturbance has occurred, as long as the nature and extent of the disturbance are fully described. Again, such important information should be located in the main data file that contains the measurements.

These recommendations echo those of others and apply to the design of long-term studies as well as the maintenance of existing records. To quote Curtis and Marshall in their excellent handbook of procedures, "Long-term permanent-plot data are often analyzed by someone other than the original investigator. Analytical techniques and objectives change over time, and there can be no certainty that the computational procedures and analyses foreseen at the time the plots were established will be those judged most suitable at the time of later analyses" (2005: p. 9).

Existing long-term data sets from experiments conducted at EFRs represent a treasure trove of opportunities to address contemporary problems and lessons at the scales of landscapes and regions. This treasure is at risk, but we can preserve it by developing a central and consistent database for all long-term studies, both past and present. Many examples exist; Poage and Anderson (2007) cataloged 12 large-scale silviculture experiments in the Pacific Northwest and developed a relational database with a number of data matrices. Other models include the Long Term Ecological Research network and the Ameriflux network, both of which require that investigators input critical metadata into a central system. Such a system would not only safeguard current studies, preventing the documentation problem from continuing, but would also provide a repository for data from earlier studies that could be included as time and resources permit.

In conclusion, locating, cataloging, and documenting data sets require a great deal of commitment and effort, both of which must be sustained over time. As stated by Pitt and Lanteigne, "The long and continued efforts of a number of field and office personnel over the years have kept this study 'alive' and the data in sound form to permit our analyses." (2008: p. 607) Although not every study may be useful for future research, the time spent identifying and updating long-term studies that are good candidates for synthesis, retrospective analysis, or reopening is an investment that can provide excellent returns, both now and in the future.

Acknowledgments

Many thanks to Connie Harrington, William Leak, Mike Shelton, and Dan Yaussy for providing the data used for this study and for patiently answering my many questions. Elizabeth LaPoint provided the map used in figure 1, and Susan Stout supplied the inspiration for the study. The manuscript benefited greatly from Linda Heath's thoughtful review and comments from Susan Stout. Thanks to all who participated in the survey and to Mary Beth Adams for convening the Experimental Forests and Ranges Synthesis Workshop.

Literature Cited

Adams, M.B.; Loughry, L.; Plaugher, L., comps. 2008. Experimental forests and ranges of the USDA Forest Service. Gen. Tech. Rep. NE-321 Revised. [CD ROM] Newtown Square, PA: U.S. Department of Agriculture, Forest Service, Northeastern Research Station. 178 p. http://nrs fs fed.us/pubs/6741. (28 January).

Burger, J.A.; Powers, R.F. 1991. Field designs for testing hypotheses in long-term site productivity studies. In: Dyck, W.W.; Mees, C.A., eds. Long-term field trials to assess environmental impacts of harvesting. Proceedings, IEA/BE T6/A6 workshop. IEA/BE T6/A6 Rep. No. 5. FRI Bulletin No. 161. Rotorua, New Zealand: Forest Research Institute: 79–105.

Cain, M.D.; Shelton, M.G. 2001. Natural loblolly and shortleaf pine productivity through 53 years of management under four reproduction cutting methods. Southern Journal of Applied Forestry. 25: 7–16.

Curtis, R.O.; Marshall, D.D. 2005. Permanent-plot procedures for silvicultural and yield research. Gen. Tech. Rep. PNW-634. Portland, OR: U.S. Department of Agriculture, Forest Service, Pacific Northwest Research Station. 86 p.

Dolph, K.L.; Mori, S.R.; Oliver, W.W. 1995. Long-term response of old-growth stands to varying levels of partial cutting in the eastside pine type. Western Journal of Applied Forestry. 10: 101–108.

Franklin, J.F.; Bledsoe, C.S.; Callahan, J.T. 1990. Contributions of the long-term ecological research program. BioScience. 40: 509–523.

Hoover, C.M.; Stout, S.L. 2007. The carbon consequences of thinning techniques: stand structure makes a difference. Journal of Forestry. 105: 266–270.

Jenkins, J.C.; Chojnacky, D.C.; Heath, L.S.; Birdsey, R.A. 2003. National-scale biomass estimators for United States tree species. Forest Science. 49: 12–35.

Lugo, A.E.; Swanson, F.J.; González, O.R., et al. 2006. Long-term research at the USDA Forest Service's experimental forests and ranges. BioScience. 56: 39–48.

Marquis, D.A. 1969. Thinning in young northern hardwoods: 5-year results. Res. Pap. NE-139. Upper Darby, PA: U.S. Department of Agriculture, Forest Service, Northeastern Forest Experiment Station. 22 p.

Marshall, J.A.; Deitschman, G.H. 1976. Computerization of data handling for long-term forest research plots. Northwest Science. 50: 231–235.

Miller, R.E.; Reukema, D.L.; Anderson, H.W. 2004. Tree growth and soil relations at the 1925 Wind River spacing test in coast Douglas fir. Res. Pap. PNW-RP-558. Portland, OR: U.S. Department of Agriculture, Forest Service, Pacific Northwest Research Station. 41 p.

Pitt, D.; Lanteigne, L. 2008. Long-term outcome of precommercial thinning in northwestern New Brunswick: growth and yield of balsam fir and red spruce. Canadian Journal of Forest Research. 38: 592–610.

Poage, N.J.; Anderson, P.D. 2007. Large-scale silviculture experiments of western Oregon and Washington. Gen. Tech. Rep. PNW-GTR-713. Portland, OR: U.S. Department of Agriculture, Forest Service, Pacific Northwest Research Station. 44 p.

Powers, R.F. 1989. Retrospective studies in perspective: strengths and weaknesses. In: Dyck, W.J.; Mees, C.A., eds. Research strategies for long-term site productivity. Proceedings, IEA/BE A3 workshop. IEA/BE A3 Rep. No. 8. FRI Bulletin No.152. Rotorua, New Zealand: Forest Research Institute: 47–62.

Powers, R.F. 1999. If you build it, will they come? Survival skills for silvicultural studies. The Forestry Chronicle. 75: 367–373.

Powers, R.F.; Mean, D.J.; Burger, J.A.; Ritchie, M.W. 1994. Designing long-term site productivity experiments. In: Dyck, W.J.; Cole, D.W.; Comerford, N.B., eds. 2004. Impacts of forest harvesting on long-term site productivity. London, United Kingdom: Chapman and Hall: 247–286.

Sanchez, F.G.; Scott, D.A.; Ludovici, K.H. 2006. Negligible effects of severe organic matter removal and soil compaction on loblolly pine growth over 10 years. Forest Ecology and Management. 227: 145–154.

Scott, D.A.; Tiarks, A.E.; Sanchez, F.G., et al. 2004. Forest soil productivity on the southern long-term soil productivity sites at age 5. In: Conner, K.F., ed. Proceedings, 12th biennial southern silvicultural research conference. Gen. Tech. Rep. SRS-71. Asheville, NC: U.S. Department of Agriculture, Forest Service, Southern Research Station: 372–377.

Smith, J.E.; Heath, L.S.; Skog, K.E.; Birdsey, R.A. 2006. Methods for calculating forest ecosystem and harvested carbon with standard estimates for forest types of the United States. Gen. Tech. Rep. NE-343. Newtown Square, PA: U.S. Department of Agriculture, Forest Service, Northeastern Research Station. 216 p.

Thomas, T.B.; Lehmkuhl, J.F.; Raphael, M.G.; DeBell, D.S. 1993. Sites for retrospective studies: opportunities for research in western Washington and Oregon. Gen. Tech. Rep. PNW-312. Portland, OR: U.S. Department of Agriculture, Forest Service, Pacific Northwest Research Station. 24 p.

Zhang, J.; Oliver, W.W.; Powers, R.F. 2005. Long-term effects of thinning and fertilization on growth of red fir in northeastern California. Canadian Journal of Forest Research. 35: 1285–1293.

Hydrologic Influences of Forest Vegetation in a Changing World: Learning From Forest Service Experimental Forests, Ranges, and Watersheds

Thomas E. Lisle[1], Mary Beth Adams[2], Leslie M. Reid[3], and Kelly Elder[4]

Abstract

The importance of forests in providing reliable sources of clean water cannot be underestimated. Therefore, there is a pressing need to understand how hydrologic systems function in forested ecosystems, in response to a variety of traditional and novel stressors and environments. Long-term watershed research on Experimental Forests and Ranges (EFRs) of the Forest Service has provided many examples of how vegetation management affects streamflows. New challenges and new stressors will require a deeper understanding and novel research and synthetic activities to help ensure sound forest management for a variety of end uses, included reliable supplies of clean water. In this paper, we discuss the potential role of EFRs for addressing new and challenging issues in forest hydrology.

Introduction

The effective management of forests requires a sound under-standing of the structure and processes of forest ecosystems and the ability to predict changes precipitated by planned and unplanned disturbances. Because silviculture provides the primary means for managing forests, there is a need to examine the effects of silvicultural activities on various forest ecosystem properties and components. One component of particular importance is water. Forest lands provide 52 percent of the U.S. drinking water as well as a high proportion of water used for agriculture; forests support abundant opportunities for water-related recreation and they provide habitat for freshwater aquatic organisms. Therefore, it is vitally important that we understand how to manage forests to sustain this role as a reliable source of high-quality water. An understanding of the influence of vegetation on streamflows can help managers plan silviculture activities to be compatible with the needs of downstream water users and of other water-related ecosystem services and values (Kochenderfer et al. 2007).

The Forest Service, U.S. Department of Agriculture (USDA), network of EFRs and experimental watersheds provides unique opportunities to improve our understanding of the effects of silviculture on hydrology. Since the early 20th century, EFRs have been sites for long-term experiments on hydrologic response to vegetation manipulation, usually involving some degree of removal and regrowth. Several thorough reviews have evaluated the hydrologic influences of forest vegetation (Bosch and Hewlett 1982, Huxman et al. 2005, NRC 2008, Stednick 1996), and much of the data those reviews rely on was provided by EFR experiments.

Most EFRs were established decades ago, and since then, new causes of vegetation change have become important, new re-sources are being threatened, and new research questions have arisen. The most prominent among these are related to global change. Shifts in climate are changing the patterns of water supply and distribution that human cultures rely on at the same time that increasing populations are creating new demands for water. Meanwhile, stresses on water-dependent resources and values are also increasing due to the cumulative influence of climatic shifts and increasing human populations. Society's

[1] Research Hydrologist, U S Department of Agriculture (USDA) Forest Service, Pacific Southwest Research Station, Redwood Sciences Laboratory, Arcata, CA

[2] Supervisory Soil Scientist, USDA Forest Service, Northern Research Station, Timber and Watershed Laboratory, Parsons, WV

[3] Research Hydrologist, USDA Forest Service, Pacific Southwest Research Station, Redwood Sciences Laboratory, Arcata, CA

[4] Supervisory Research Hydrologist, USDA Forest Service, Rocky Mountain Research Station, Fort Collins, CO

capacity to adapt to these changes will depend strongly on the ability to understand and predict future changes and to modify land management practices to compensate for those changes.

Innovative approaches for analysis and synthesis will be needed if the emerging issues in forest hydrology are to be adequately addressed at the spatial and temporal scales required. Developing an understanding of global change requires large-scale approaches. Although each EFR is relatively small, its distribution across North America enables regional- or continental-scale syntheses (Lugo et al. 2006). With the accumulation of completed studies across a variety of ecoclimatic zones, ongoing long-term data collection, and introduction of new approaches to data management, the construction of useful syntheses across continental transects is becoming increasingly feasible.

This paper discusses the potential role of EFRs for addressing new issues in forest hydrology. We first outline interactions between vegetation and hydrology to provide a context for understanding the problems, then identify issues likely to be of particular importance in coming decades, and finally describe analytical strategies that could be used to address the issues using data from EFRs.

Stand-Scale Interactions Between Vegetation and Water

In forests, vegetation influences each step in the pathway linking precipitation and runoff (fig. 1). A portion of a storm's rain or snow encounters foliage, where it may be stored until it evaporates ("interception loss"), drains as stemflow, or drips to the ground. Rates of interception loss are influenced by canopy conditions and climatic setting and can be appreciable in some forests. Second-growth redwood forests at the Caspar Creek Experimental Forest in coastal California were found to intercept and evaporate 20 to 25 percent of the annual rainfall, for example, with greater than 16-percent loss rates observed even during high-intensity storms (Reid and Lewis 2007). Interception rates tend to be lower in continental climatic settings and in hardwood forests relative to conifers. For example, estimated interception rates at Coweeta Hydrologic Laboratory ranged from a low of 2 percent of annual precipitation to 13 percent in hardwood catchments to 15 to 26 percent in white pine (Helvey and Patric 1988). In some areas, forest canopies

have been found to collect water from fog, leading to precipitation beneath the canopy during nonrain periods (Harr 1982). Discussion of rainfall interception in subalpine western forests is largely academic because the snow-dominated hydrologic regime is heavily impacted by wintertime interception and subsequent sublimation loss in these forests. Summertime interception losses are a small percentage of the annual subalpine water balance and most rainfall is consumed on site before reaching a stream.

Interception and sublimation of snow can result in significant losses of wintertime precipitation in mature subalpine forests. At the Fraser Experimental Forest, snowfall accounts for about 70 percent of the annual precipitation (Alexander et al. 1985) and more than 90 percent of the annual runoff, so canopy losses directly through sublimation represent a significant portion of the annual potential water yield. Montesi et al. (2004) gave a conservative estimate of 20- to 30-percent loss of total snowfall to sublimated interception. Studies on the effect of timber removal on water yield have shown that about one-third of the increased yield following clearcutting can be attributed to savings from canopy sublimation, while the other two-thirds can be relegated to the removal of growing season evapotranspirational losses (Troendle and King 1985).

After rainfall or snowmelt encounters the ground surface, it may infiltrate or—if input rates are greater than infiltration rates or the ground is saturated—run off across the surface

Figure 1.—*Diagram of hydrologic fluxes. The strength of the fluxes is indicated by arrow thickness and is broadly representative of a temperate forest.*

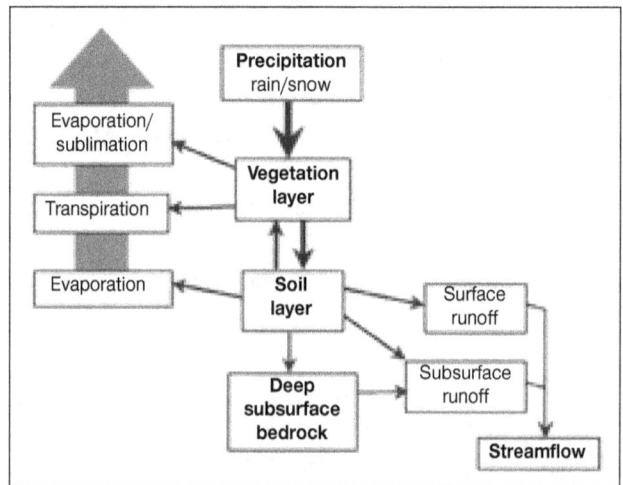

as overland flow. Infiltration is promoted by the presence of porous soils and by surficial materials, such as forest litter, that slow surface flows. Overland flow usually increases where soil is compacted and can be particularly extensive where hydrophobic soil layers are formed by fire or exposure of dry soil. Where soils have become saturated, overland flow also occurs through both exfiltration and direct precipitation onto the saturated area. Increased rates of overland flow often generate high erosion rates and increased peak flows, increasing storm runoff at the expense of long-term moisture storage on hillslopes. Vegetation strongly influences soil structure, organic content, litter composition, and the generation of hydrophobic soil conditions, and so can affect the distribution of overland flow.

Water that infiltrates into the soil becomes available for uptake by roots and evaporation through transpiration. Uptake and transpiration rates vary considerably by species, season, and stand age. Rates are generally highest during seasons of maximum growth, and riparian stands tend to sustain high transpiration rates both because species with high water-use requirements grow there and because water is consistently available for transpiration near streams. Soils with high water storage potential—deep soils and those rich in clays or organic matter—can support higher rates of transpiration for longer periods between storms. At a given site, soil moisture is more rapidly depleted between storms when transpiration rates are high, increasing the volume available for moisture storage at the onset of the next storm and thus reducing the potential for overland flow during the storm. Transpiration accounts for about 25 percent of the annual precipitation in the redwood forest at the Caspar Creek Experimental Forest (Reid and Lewis 2007), while potential evapotranspiration is about 51 percent of precipitation in the mixed deciduous hardwood forests at the Fernow Experimental Forest (Adams et al. 1994). Kaufmann (1985) showed large differences between tree species in the central Rocky Mountains; however, average values of around 50 percent of annual precipitation consumed by evapotranspiration agree with those values of Leaf (1975).

Water draining downward through soil or fractured bedrock during and immediately after storms may be diverted to flow downslope along less-permeable horizons and so reach streams, adding to stormflows already enhanced by overland flow inputs and by direct precipitation into the streams. The remaining water eventually reaches the water table and accumulates as ground water. Streamflow between storms and during dry seasons is sustained through the drainage of ground water. At Caspar Creek, about 50 percent of the annual rainfall of 1,165 mm reappears as streamflow, with 63 percent of the flow occurring as stormflow. The Caspar Creek forest thus strongly influences the disposition of one-half the annual precipitation through interception and transpiration and also affects the relative importance of baseflow and stormflow through its influence on hillslope flow paths during storms. At Fernow Experimental Forest, streamflow averages 710 mm per year, or about 48 percent of precipitation. Fool Creek in Fraser Experimental Forest had a pretreatment runoff efficiency of about 37 percent with 760 mm precipitation and 280 mm streamflow (Goodell 1958). South-facing basins at Fraser tend to produce more runoff with close to 50-percent efficiency. These values vary locally with aspect and elevation of individual basins but are generally representative.

Water flowing through streams is also strongly influenced by forest vegetation. Riparian vegetation moderates stream temperatures through shading, and large woody debris not only provides habitat for aquatic biota but also modifies channel hydraulics by increasing channel roughness. Flow slows in debris-laden reaches, increasing in-channel storage of water and sediment and hyporheic exchange including nutrients.

Interactions between hydrology and forest vegetation are by no means unidirectional. Forest species composition, growth rates, and susceptibility to environmental stresses are strongly influenced by the availability of water and nutrients that are primarily stored in soils. For example, sugar maple growing on summit and upslope sites in northwestern Pennsylvania, with poorer nutrient and moisture status, were more likely to demonstrate decline symptoms than those growing in more moisture- and nutrient-rich toeslope positions (Horsley et al. 2000).

Emerging Issues Regarding Forests and Water

Past issues in forest hydrology centered primarily on the effects of logging on water yield, flooding, and water quality, with the intent of reducing impacts to domestic water supplies and downstream infrastructure. Now attention is shifting to new causes of vegetative change, such as air pollution, invasive exotic species, introduced pathogens, and climate change, and to different downstream resources, such as ecosystem integrity. The influences of forests on hydrology are known mainly from small-scale experiments carried out over relatively short periods (NRC 2008), but relationships between intensities of vegetative stress and magnitudes and durations of hydrologic response now need to be evaluated at larger temporal and spatial scales if the kinds of hydrologic influences that occur over the landscape are to be adequately understood.

Many new stressors, such as climate change and exotic pathogens, are lower in intensity than some direct land use practices but are more pervasive and represent chronic disturbances. Climate change alters the effects of land use and disturbances on ecosystem processes and services and requires managers to evaluate and manage for cumulative impacts in new ways to take these influences into account. Because of the scales over which the chronic disturbances act, impact predictions now need to address the basin or landscape scale and must encompass time scales for impact expression that are far longer than have been evaluated in the past.

Global climatic change can alter the volume, timing, and type of precipitation, which, in turn, can influence vegetation. Shallow snowpacks may begin melting earlier in the spring and melt more rapidly, leading to increased peak flows and creating prolonged summer drought. Warmer temperatures may foster the spread of pathogens and insect pests that otherwise are suppressed by cold winters (Negron and Popp 2004). Wildfires may increase in size and frequency (Westerling et al. 2006), altering vegetation and soils and further influencing the amount and quality of runoff. A change in climate can alter the availability of soil moisture and modify forest disturbance patterns, leading to pervasive changes in forest species composition and age distribution. Influences on the hydrologic regime are then compounded, reflecting both the climate shift and the change in vegetation.

Increased human populations at the wildland-urban interface modify both the potential for wildfire and the strategies used to fight wildfires and often entail increased water extractions from wildland streams. Increased populations are also associated with increased atmospheric deposition of contaminants in particulate or dissolved form and with increased concentrations of gaseous constituents of smog. Atmospheric deposition and

exposure to smog can affect vegetative health and its ability to perform hydrologic functions (Schaberg et al. 2000), and atmospheric constituents may accumulate in soils and affect water quality (Driscoll et al. 2001). Any changes in environmental conditions that influence the health and distribution of forest vegetation can potentially alter the volume, timing, and quality of runoff from forest lands.

In addition, human influences on hydrology are becoming more complex as new impacts increasingly overlie previous impacts. For example, we may understand the short-term effects of clearcutting on forest land hydrology; however, there is little research on the hydrologic effects of repeated harvesting. Several studies suggest that the hydrologic response to repeated disturbance differs from that for a single disturbance (Adams and Kochenderfer, in press; Hornbeck et al. 1993), and that some kinds of disturbances have very long recovery times (Compton et al. 1998).

In a recent review of the current state of knowledge in forest hydrology, the National Research Council (NRC 2008) identified high-priority questions that need to be answered if emerging issues are to be adequately addressed (table 1). Answering questions such as these will require considerable interdisciplinary cooperation and must involve a wide variety of research approaches. Notable as an underlying theme across the range of questions is the need for increased understanding of hydrological responses at larger spatial and temporal scales than usually have been addressed in the past.

Applying EFR Research To Address Emerging Issues in Forest Hydrology

The Forest Service EFR network appears to be uniquely positioned to provide the kinds of information needed to address issues at large spatial and temporal scales due to the existence of long-term data from the sites, the multidisciplinary breadth of research topics explored at such sites, and the diverse climates and physiographies sampled by the network (Lugo et al. 2006). Although EFRs are distributed widely across the Nation, most are small relative to the bioregional and physiographic provinces they represent. If information from EFRs is to contribute to broad-scale integrated analyses, innovative strategies for synthesis will need to be applied.

Table 1.—*Key questions regarding emerging issues in forest hydrology (from NRC 2008).*

1. What are the magnitude and duration of hydrologic effects due to timber harvest?

2. What are the hydrologic effects of removing or retaining riparian forests over the long term and in large watersheds?

3. What are the cumulative watershed effects of forest cover loss in large watersheds?

4. How do past forest cutting patterns affect water quantity and quality?

5. How have changes in grazing of both domestic and native grazers affected forests, and what are the indirect effects of those changes on water quantity and quality?

6. How do the legacies of road networks on forest land affect peak flows and sediment movement?

7. What are the hydrologic effects of forest fires and firefighting (such as fire breaks, soil disturbance, and application of fire retardants)? What are the hydrologic effects of high- versus low-severity fires, including considerations of long-term effects and larger spatial scales?

8. How do insect outbreaks affect water quantity and quality? How can future hydrologic effects of insect outbreaks be understood or predicted as indirect effects of climate change?

9. What are the hydrologic effects of nonnative species' presence and nonnative species' removal treatments in forests?

10. What are the hydrologic responses to climate change?

11. How do changes in ownership affect forest management, and how do these changes affect water resources?

12. What are the effects of the expansion of human settlements into forested areas and the consequent changes in forest management, such as thinning for fuel reduction, on water quantity and quality?

Use of Process-Based Understanding

Fundamental to all synthesis strategies is the establishment of a sound understanding of process mechanisms. Our current level of understanding of hydrologic process has been produced largely through studies carried out at the scale of laboratory benches, study plots, hillslopes, and small instrumented watersheds. EFRs have been the location of many such studies.

EFRs have been particularly useful in providing sites for paired-basin research. Such work allows controlled experiments to be carried out at spatial scales that encompass a range of site conditions, permitting the implications of site-specific process-based information to be tested in settings where a realistic array of potential influences is present. Work at the

paired-basin scale provides the basis for our ability to predict streamflow responses to vegetation changes. Because paired-basin studies require that relatively large tracts of land be set aside expressly for experimental manipulation over lengthy periods, such work is rarely feasible on lands not managed by public agencies. Even land managed by agencies must often be protected by an explicit charter prioritizing its purpose for research activities. As a result, much of our basic understanding of watershed responses to vegetation change in U.S. forests applies to conditions represented by EFRs.

Extrapolating results from EFRs to other areas requires knowledge of system performance. An EFR offers a reference not so much because it represents a certain stand condition (e.g., old growth) but because enough knowledge has been acquired at such sites to develop an understanding of how particular components of the system function and of how those components affect one another (Lisle et al. 2007). Knowledge of system performance improves the ability to transfer research results to other areas having different landscape histories and background conditions. For example, to predict how peak runoff will respond to fire in a particular area, one might seek information from EFRs that brackets the background conditions of the area of interest, but interpolation between the outcomes at those EFRs would not be sufficient to solve the problem. Rather, analysis would rely on the understanding of how peak runoff is generated at each EFR and how vegetation and fire affect peak flow generation processes. Responses for the site in question would then be estimated according to the extent to which controlling variables at that site are likely to produce the outcomes observed at the EFRs. The value of the research is not only related to the outcome of the site-specific study but also more importantly to the knowledge gained of the processes involved.

The application of process-based understanding for predicting hydrologic responses requires interdisciplinary efforts because no part of the hydrologic system is isolated from direct or indirect influences of biological systems. Understanding of hydrologic outcomes of either acute or chronic forest disturbances first requires an understanding of the initial vegetation response. At that point, it becomes possible to determine which components shown in figure 1 will be directly or indirectly affected by the change and to assess how changes in those components will influence the response of others. A greater understanding and transferability is gained by analyzing system function than by simply comparing inputs (precipitation) and outputs (runoff).

Use of Cross-Site Comparisons

The utility of paired-basin studies is increased when results are compared at multiple sites. Such work allows evaluation of hydrologic response patterns at scales much broader than those of the original experiments.

As an illustration of this approach, consider an example from three experimental forests within the Appalachians: Hubbard Brook, Fernow, and Coweeta. All three sites are mountainous watersheds dominated mostly by hardwood forests, and the paired watershed approach has been used to evaluate the hydrologic responses to clearcutting at each site (Hornbeck et al. 1997, Kochenderfer et al. 1990, Swank et al. 2001). The responses of annual water yield to clearcutting were qualitatively similar among the three sites (fig. 2). In each case, short-term increases in annual water yield were observed immediately after clearcutting, and these increases rapidly declined to or below pretreatment levels as natural revegetation of the site progressed, generally requiring less than 10 years before the differences between pretreatment and posttreatment were not statistically significant. This reduction was then followed by an increase to levels slightly greater than pretreatment. Although the general shape of the curves is common to all sites, the intercepts and the levels of the minimum flow differ among sites.

Hornbeck et al. (1997) ascribed the decrease in predicted flow at Hubbard Brook to the presence of pioneer species such as pin cherry (*Prunus pensylvanica* L.) in the regrowing forest. Pin cherry has lower rates of stomatal resistance and higher rates of transpiration than some tree species present before treatment, so streamflow was reduced while pin cherry was present. Pin cherry is a relatively short-lived species, however, and flow then began to increase as the pin cherry was replaced by maple and other later successional species. A similar explanation was offered for the responses at Coweeta and Fernow (Kochenderfer and Lee 1973, Swank et al. 2001), but the early successional species differ at those sites, with black cherry (*Prunus serotina* L.) most common at Fernow and black locust (*Robinia pseudoacacia* L.) most common at Coweeta. The differences in hydrologic responses shown in figure 2 thus are likely to reflect the different successional pathways. Such results suggest that information on species composition and successional trajectories might provide a basis for predicting hydrologic responses to management activities over wide portions of the Appalachians. Results may also be applicable to predicting effects of climate change because climate change is expected to provoke shifts in species composition in eastern hardwood forests (Iverson and Prasad 2001).

Figure 2.—*Deviation from predicted annual water yields after clearcutting Appalachian watersheds on the Fernow Experimental Forest (FEF), Hubbard Brook Experimental Forest (HB), and Coweeta Hydrologic Laboratory (CHL).*

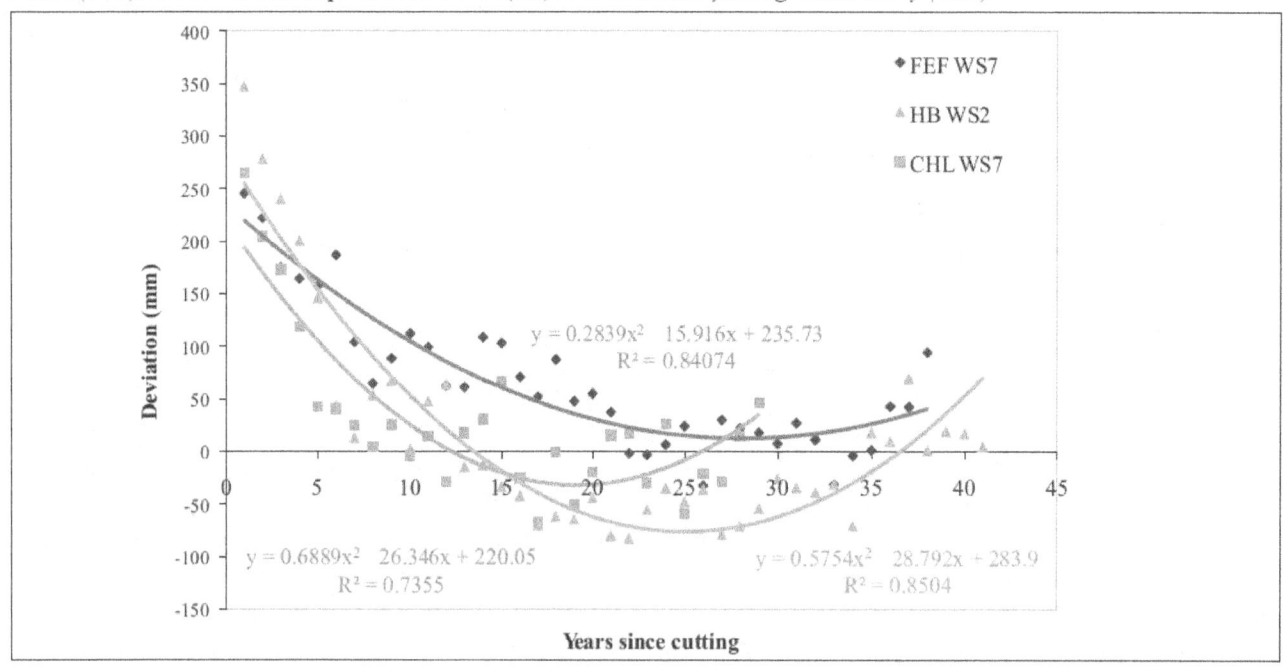

At the regional or continental scale, Jones and Post (2004) carried out cross-site comparisons of EFRs in Pacific Northwest coniferous forests and eastern hardwood forests to explore the seasonal effects of logging on streamflow and to evaluate the influence of forest age on the hydrologic response. They reported that both relative and absolute streamflow changes after forest removal were significantly and positively related to the age of the forest at the time it was cut, although there were some differences among coniferous and hardwood forests.

Using Experimental Results To Explore Unprecedented Changes

In some cases, shifts in climate or land use may alter hydrologic regimes beyond the range of responses observable in a region. Experimental manipulation of vegetation at EFRs may reveal the potential for major shifts in process regimes in response to pervasively altered conditions. A vegetation conversion experiment at the San Dimas Experimental Forest, for example, demonstrated that hillslopes there are considerably less stable under grassland than under the native chaparral vegetation (Orme and Bailey 1970). Such results suggest that climatic shifts or land use changes that expand grasslands in the area may well be accompanied by major changes in sediment regime.

The structure of the EFR network permits an additional strategy for exploring responses to unprecedented conditions. By substituting space for time, information from a larger area can be used to expand the range of variation considered. Attention must be paid, however, to the role of background variables that govern basic process relations. Comparisons across regions are most likely to be valid when variation between important background variables is minimized or when their influence can be accurately evaluated. If the disturbance is both catastrophic and ubiquitous, then the signal-to-noise ratio of well-designed studies is high and site differences may be ignored to some degree to extrapolate or interpolate important results. The current epidemic of mountain pine beetle across western North America is a good example. More than 90 percent of the lodgepole pine (*Pinus contorta* Douglas ex Louden) trees in many basins are dead or dying. With impact of this magnitude, there may be hydrologic impacts or lessons learned that are applicable across wide areas, regardless of significant site differences.

Making Use of Geographic Gradients

Small changes in climatic conditions may have disproportionate effects on forest species composition, so changes to the hydrologic regime may be far greater than those expected solely from the direct influences of the climatic shift. Resulting changes from biophysical interactions are difficult to predict, but comparing vegetation, hydrology, and their interactions across carefully selected continental gradients can provide realistic scenarios of the effects of climate change. Because of their wide distribution, EFRs provide important data sources for gradient analysis.

As an example, one critical gradient reflects the range of precipitation that causes water to be stored in the rooting zone of soils (Huxman et al. 2005). If vegetation can tap this water long enough to produce growth, precipitation will strongly influence productivity, and interception and transpiration by plants will strongly influence runoff. The critical range in which this interaction varies steeply with precipitation is in semiarid climates. In arid climates, overland flow is the only contribution to surface flow during intense precipitation. Vegetation is sparse and has little influence on surface runoff. In wet climates lacking a seasonal drought, vegetation generally has more water than it can use, so variations in precipitation do not affect plant growth, and plants transpire the same amount of water regardless of precipitation. Climatic changes that shift rainfall into the critical range would entail much stronger hydrologic and vegetation responses than would climatic changes of similar magnitude in drier or wetter contexts. In this case, an understanding of the nature of the gradient would allow the prediction of nonlinear hydrologic responses. The presence of EFRs across this gradient enables a space-for-time approach to this problem.

In other cases, gradient analysis provides a basis for broad-scale extrapolations by defining ranges of variability of attributes across large areas. A series of experimental watersheds is distributed along the Pacific Coast from San Dimas in Southern California to near Juneau in Alaska (fig. 3). Annual precipitation increases from 700 mm at San Dimas to 4,000 mm on Vancouver Island, then decreases again to about 2,500 mm near Juneau. Foliar interception of rainfall has been measured in coniferous forests at or near four of these sites, and average interception in each area was found to be between 22 and 32 percent of annual rainfall, irrespective of the amount of rain. The consistency of interception rates across this broad climatic gradient provides reasonable assurance that similar values might be expected in similar mature coastal coniferous forests along the sampled gradient. The shifts in conifer species composition that might be expected from a climate change thus are unlikely to cause large changes in interception loss in mature Coast Range forests. Measurements at the San Dimas Experimental Forest, however, show annual interception losses of 7.9 percent in grassland and 12.8 percent in chaparral (Corbett and Crouse 1968), suggesting that climatic or land use changes strong enough to cause a change in cover type might induce a strong shift in hydrologic regime.

Another critical climate-related gradient exists in areas with seasonal snowpacks. EFRs spanning a wide elevation range, such as the Fraser Experimental Forest, or multiple sites spanning a latitudinal range, such as the Fraser, Tenderfoot,

and Priest River Experimental Forests, all offer possibilities for examining the role of climate in snow-dominated hydrologic regimes. The Fraser site shows no statistically significant change in annual mean or daily maximum temperature at low elevation (2,750 m at sea level); however, daily minimum annual temperature does show a significant increase (Elder and Porth, unpublished data, fig. 4). (As an aside, this temperature record may be valuable in quantifying causal factors related to the current mountain pine beetle epidemic, which is having a profound impact on Fraser area forests.) Long-term runoff records from Fraser Experimental Forest gauged watersheds show that daily maximum discharge and instantaneous peak flow are occurring a week to 10 days earlier when post-1985 data are compared to historical pre-1985 records, with some variation depending on physiography and historic land use (logging). Records also show no change in high-elevation snow accumulation (fig. 5) but show a decrease at the lowest elevation snow course (fig. 6). All these details are interesting

Figure 3.—*Variation of annual foliar interception and annual precipitation along a latitudinal gradient on the Pacific coast of North America. Letters identify research watersheds. All watersheds except San Dimas are dominated by coniferous forests.*

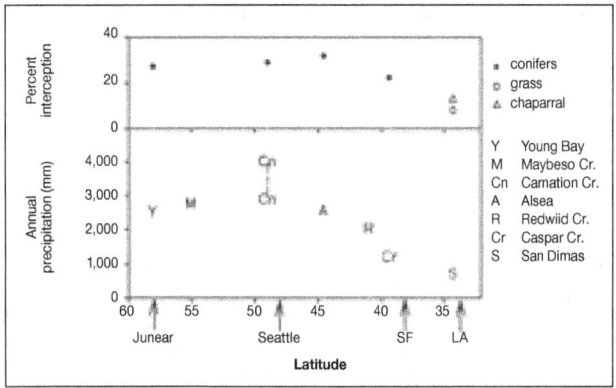

Figure 4.—*Year of observation versus temperature. T_{max} is the warmest mean daily temperature for a given year. T_{min} is the coldest mean daily temperature for a given year, and T_{mean} is the mean temperature for the entire year indicated.*

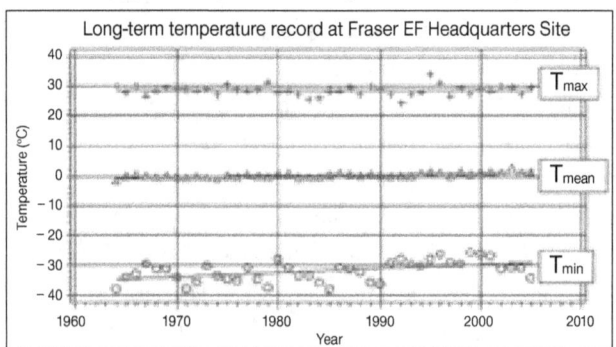

Figure 5.—*Year of occurrence versus mean peak water equivalent as measured on Fool Creek snow courses with fitted regression lines.*

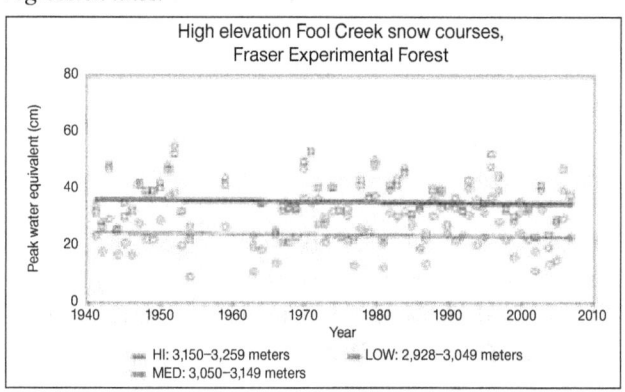

Figure 6.—*Year of occurrence versus mean peak water equivalent with fitted regression lines.*

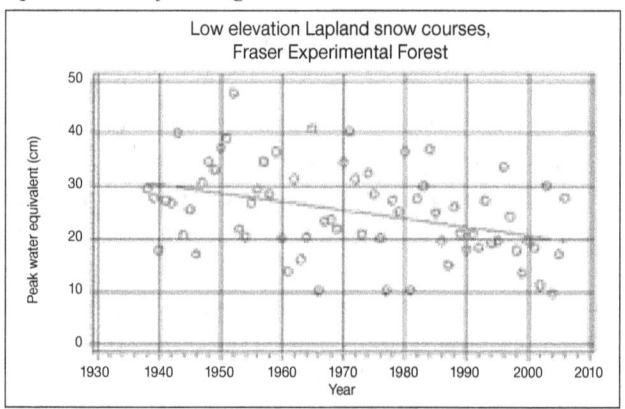

by themselves, but the individual experimental forests and the EFR network provide the possibility of quantifying the effects while learning the causes. Learning the causes may mean quantifying processes, statistically relating independent and dependent relationships, developing useful empirical relationships, or even developing deterministic models capable of predicting observations or as-of-yet unobserved outcomes. Indeed, researchers are attracted to EFRs for model development, testing, and application as evidenced by the history of hydrological models partially developed at the Fraser Experimental Forest alone. These models include WATBAL (Leaf and Brink 1973), WRENS (Troendle and Leaf 1980), MicroMet (Liston and Elder 2006a), SnowModel (Liston and Elder 2006b), SnowAssim (Liston and Hiemstra 2008), and FASST and SNTHERM (Frankenstein et al. 2008).

Developing Latent Experiments by Using Long-Term Records

Because of the long history of experimental work at currently active EFRs and at those operated in the past, many opportunities exist to revisit the outcomes of previous research. At a minimum, such work can be valuable for extending the length of record to allow assessment of long-term recovery rates. As an example, the Alsea Experimental Watersheds of coastal Oregon were initially monitored between 1959 and 1973, with monitoring continuing long enough after the 1966 logging for researchers to conclude that hydrologic recovery from logging was nearly complete. The monitoring network was reestablished in 1990, and subsequent measurements demonstrated that the hydrologic regime had, in fact, *not* yet returned to pretreatment conditions (Stednick et al. 2006). Such sites also provide an opportunity to evaluate the effects of superimposing modern activities on the legacy conditions left by well-documented earlier experimental treatments.

Finally, EFRs sometimes produce surprises when functioning as observatories. Experiments and studies are designed to test hypotheses by measuring the variation of certain variables with enough time and precision to observe the effects of imposed changes or natural variability. Unexpected payoffs may accrue, however, especially if basic variables describing system functions are measured over long periods, when unusual events occur, new functional relations are discovered, or new ques-

tions arise. For example, interactions between woody debris and riparian forests were observed during a large flood at the H.J. Andrews Experimental Forest (Johnson et al. 2000). Sediment monitoring at Caspar Creek Experimental Forest has revealed a pulse of sediment caused by disturbances from logging that occurred three decades ago.

Expanding Applications of EFR Information

Although EFRs are themselves limited in area, they are usually embedded in much larger tracts of public lands. Even though the larger land base cannot be managed as a controlled experiment, the combination of the process-based understanding gained from EFR experiments with the records of treatments applied to the surrounding areas can be used to develop retrospective predictions of outcomes at the larger scale (Lisle et al. 2007). These predictions can then be tested through observation of current conditions at the larger scale. As references where system functions are relatively well understood, EFRs can be used to understand variations in ecosystem processes and conditions in managed watersheds that are subject to a wide range of disturbances. A reference framework can evolve as "client" watersheds accumulate information and contribute to the understanding initially anchored by reference watersheds or EFRs.

The infrastructure (meteorological stations, stream gauges, vegetation data, spatial data, etc.) existing at EFRs is unparalleled in potential to ask and answer timely, critical scientific and management-oriented questions through the development of process models and similar predictive tools. Hydrologic models, like atmospheric models, are very often used to forecast a particular outcome; e.g., timing and volume of runoff, peak flows, ground water levels, etc. Modelers and scientists often begin development using a single location or system. If a model is successful for that single system, then the modeler begins looking for ways to improve its performance, searching for other applications for the model, or attempts to make it more universal. The latter approach involves making the model more deterministic, or further parameterizing independent variables to fit more potential cases. EFRs offer the potential to help modelers and scientists in all these efforts. Many EFRs have long-term data, which allows modelers to look at variability over time—an important component of any model in terms of efficacy and model stability. EFRs also offer a broad variety of records of independent variables that may be useful for many different applications. Climate data is a good example: climate data from the Fraser Experimental Forest have recently been used for hydrological, biogeochemical, ecological, geomorphological, entomological, silvicultural, remote sensing, atmospheric dynamics, and climatological modeling.

Some examples provide evidence for the argument described previously. The Simultaneous Heat And Water (SHAW) model (Flerchinger and Saxton 1989a, 1989b) was largely developed at the Reynolds Creek Experimental Watershed, near Boise, ID (operated by the USDA Agricultural Research Service), which is characterized by arid rangelands with limited forest cover, typical of many midelevation watersheds in the West. The model proved valuable under these conditions and the developers began looking for ways to expand its applicability. In a radical departure from an arid midelevation basin, SHAW was modified and successfully applied to a low-elevation coastal forest at the H.J. Andrews Experimental Forest (Link et al. 2004). Flerchinger also was able to adapt the model to subalpine hillslopes at Fraser Experimental Forest, with some modifications for slope and canopy (Goodbody 2004). In all, there have been more than 40 papers written on the SHAW model and its utility to a wide variety of hydrologic environments and physiographies.

In its earliest incantations, SnowModel (Liston and Elder 2006b) was developed to model snow transport in an arctic environment. Again, the needs of Liston and other users drove an effort to expand the model's applicability over a wider range of the Earth's surface. Fraser Experimental Forest offered an opportunity to work in a forested environment where the effects of trees on radiation, wind, and interception and sublimation on snow processes could be intensively quantified. Existing infrastructure and long-term data (runoff, climate, silviculture), and contemporary data at high spatial and temporal resolutions (four-component radiation, interception, snowmelt, etc.) were available to drive the model under the most likely demanding uses. SnowModel has now been applied from Greenland to Antarctica and across a wide range of environments in between.

Snow Model Intercomparison Project 2 (SnowMIP2) was a research effort designed to compare existing snow process models and evaluate the effect of forests on their performance.

In all, 33 models were tested by a large group of researchers using data sets from five sites. Models were submitted from scientists worldwide. Study sites and data sets were chosen from a worldwide pool of sites. Fraser Experimental Forest was one of the sites selected, due to the qualities mentioned previously. The results are published in Rutter et al. (2009), and the model evaluation work will prove valuable to scientists and those seeking to apply the best available model for their particular situation.

Conclusions

Interactions between vegetation and hydrology are fundamental ecosystem processes that govern the health of the Nation's forests and water supplies. These interactions have been studied intensively in the past, yet they deserve even more attention now as scientists grapple with the crucial problems presented by global change. Solutions will require integrating knowledge across a range of scale from the plant to the continent. In this range, process-based information is rich, deep, and widespread at the scale of stands or small watersheds, thanks to the operation of a network of experimental forests, ranges, and watersheds over many decades.

The pace of change and our limited ability to deflect trajectories influenced by management, including silviculture, means that we can ill afford to rely on adaptive management at a large scale to avoid problems compounded by global change. Instead, we must also use available information and models to predict the consequences of management as best we can. In this regard, EFRs provide an important role as observatories of vegetative and hydrologic phenomena, sites for controlled experiments imposing disturbance even wider in range than those imposed under present conditions, and interdisciplinary studies that inform models of ecosystem functions. Although small in area, EFRs represent a wide range of ecosystems and are strategically located to enable syntheses across continental-scale gradients. Examples of syntheses sketched out in this paper illustrate a potential to greatly enhance the latent value of data from EFRs that has accumulated over decades without an appreciation for its role in problems of the magnitude of global change.

Literature Cited

Adams, M.B.; Kochenderfer, J.N. [In press]. Recovery of central Appalachian forested watersheds: comparison of Fernow and Coweeta results. In: Swank, W.T.; Webster, J.R., eds. Long-term response of a forest watershed ecosystem: clearcutting in the southern Appalachians. New York: Springer.

Adams, M.B.; Kochenderfer, J.N.; Wood, F., et al. 1994. Forty years of hydrometeorological data from the Fernow Experimental Forest, West Virginia. Gen. Tech. Rep. NE-184. Radnor, PA: U.S. Department of Agriculture, Forest Service, Northeastern Forest Experiment Station. 24 p.

Alexander, R.; Troendle, C.; Kaufmann, M., et al. 1985. The Fraser Experimental Forest, Colorado: research program and published research, 1937–1985. Gen. Tech. Rep. RM-118. Fort Collins, CO: U.S. Department of Agriculture, Forest Service, Rocky Mountain Forest and Range Experiment Station. 46 p.

Bosch, J.M.; Hewlett, J.D. 1982. A review of catchment experiments to determine the effect of vegetation changes on water yield and evapotranspiration. Journal of Hydrology. 55: 3–23.

Compton, J.E.; Boone, R.D.; Motzkin, G.; Foster, D.R. 1998. Soil carbon and nitrogen in a pine-oak sand plain in central Massachusetts: role of vegetation and land-use history. Oecologia. 116: 536–642.

Corbett, E.S.; Crouse, R.P. 1968. Rainfall interception by annual grass and chaparral...losses compared. Res. Pap. PSW-48. Berkeley, CA: U.S. Department of Agriculture, Forest Service, Pacific Southwest Forest and Range Experiment Station. 12 p.

Driscoll, C.T.; Lawrence, G.B.; Bulger, A.H., et al. 2001. Acidic deposition in the Northeastern United States: source and inputs, ecosystem effects and management strategies. BioScience. 51(3): 180–198.

Elder, K.J.; Porth, L.S. 2009. Unpublished data. On file with: Aquatic and Riparian Ecosystems Project, Rocky Mountain Research Station, Fort Collins, CO.

Flerchinger, G.N.; Saxton, K.E. 1989a. Simultaneous heat and water model of a freezing snow-residue-soil system. I. Theory and development. Transactions of the American Society of Agricultural Engineering. 32(2): 565–571.

Flerchinger, G.N.; Saxton, K.E. 1989b. Simultaneous heat and water model of a freezing snow-residue-soil system. II. Field verification. Transactions of the American Society of Agricultural Engineering. 32(2): 573–578.

Frankenstein, S.; Sawyer, A.; Koeberle, J. 2008. Comparison of FASST and SNTHERM in three snow accumulation regimes. Journal of Hydrometeorology. 9(6): 1443–1463.

Goodbody, A. 2004. Soil heat and water model validation during snowmelt in a mature forest and regenerating clearcut on a Colorado subalpine hillslope. Fort Collins, CO: Colorado State University, Department of Earth Resources. M.S. thesis.

Goodell, B. 1958. A preliminary report on the first year's effects of timber harvesting on water yield from a Colorado watershed. Sta. Pap. No. 36. Fort Collins, CO: U.S. Department of Agriculture, Forest Service, Rocky Mountain Forest and Range Experiment Station. 12 p.

Harr, R.D. 1982. Fog drip in the Bull Run municipal watershed, Oregon. Water Resources Bulletin. 78(5): 785–789.

Helvey, J.D.; Patric, J.H. 1988. Research on interception losses and soil moisture relationship. In: Swank, W.T.; Crossley, D.A., Jr., eds. Forest hydrology and ecology and Coweeta. New York: Springer-Verlag: 129–137.

Hornbeck, J.W.; Adams, M.B.; Corbett, E.S., et al. 1993. Long-term impacts of forest treatments on water yield: a summary for the Northeastern USA. Journal of Hydrology. 150: 323–344.

Hornbeck, J.W.; Martin, C.W.; Eagar, C. 1997. Summary of water yield experiments at Hubbard Brook Experimental Forest, New Hampshire. Canadian Journal of Forest Research. 27: 2043–2052.

Horsley, S.B.; Long, R.B.; Bailey, S.B., et al. 2000. Factors associated with the decline disease of sugar maple on the Allegheny Plateau. Canadian Journal of Forest Research. 30: 1365–1378.

Huxman, T.E.; Wilcox, B.P.; Breshears, D.D., et al. 2005. Ecohydrological implications of woody plant encroachment. Ecology. 86: 308–319.

Iverson, L.R.; Prasad, A.M. 2001. Potential changes in tree species richness and forest community types following climate change. Ecosystems. 4: 186–199.

Johnson, S.L.; Swanson, F.J.; Grant, G.E.; Wondzell, S.M. 2000. Riparian forest disturbances by a mountain flood—the influence of floated wood. Hydrological Processes. 14: 3031–3050.

Jones, J.A.; Post, D.A. 2004. Seasonal and successional stream-flow response to forest cutting and regrowth in the Northwest and Eastern United States. Water Resources Research. (40) WO5203, doi:10.1029/2003WR002952.

Kaufmann, M.R. 1985. Annual transpiration in subalpine forests: large differences among four tree species. Forest Ecology and Management. 13: 235–246.

Kochenderfer, J.N.; Adams, M.B.; Miller, G.W.; Helvey, J.D. 2007. Factors affecting large peakflows on Appalachian watersheds: lessons from the Fernow Experimental Forest. Res. Pap. NRS-3. Newtown Square, PA: U.S. Department of Agriculture, Forest Service, Northern Research Station. 24 p.

Kochenderfer, J.N.; Edwards, P.J.; Helvey, J.D. 1990. Land management and water yield in the Appalachians. In: Proceedings, watershed planning and analysis in action symposium. Reston, VA: American Society of Civil Engineers, IR Division: 523–532.

Kochenderfer, J.N.; Lee, R. 1973. Indexes to transpiration by forest trees. Oecologica Plantarum. 8(2): 175–184.

Leaf, C.F. 1975. Watershed management in the Rocky Mountain subalpine zone: the status of our knowledge. Res. Pap. RM-137. Fort Collins, CO: U.S. Department of Agriculture, Forest Service, Rocky Mountain Forest and Range Experiment Station. 31 p.

Leaf, C.F.; Brink, G.E. 1973. Hydrologic simulation model of Colorado subalpine forest. Res. Pap. RM-107. Fort Collins, CO: U.S. Department of Agriculture, Forest Service, Rocky Mountain Forest and Range Experiment Station. 23 p.

Link, T.E.; Flerchinger, G.N.; Unsworth, M.H.; Marks, D. 2004. Simulation of water and energy fluxes in an old growth seasonal temperate rainforest using the simultaneous heat and water (SHAW) model. Journal of Hydrometeorology. 5(3): 443–457.

Lisle, T.E.; Cummins, K.; Madej, M.A. 2007. An examination of references for ecosystems in a watershed context: results of a scientific pulse in Redwood National and State Parks, California. In: Furniss, M.; Clifton, C.F.; Ronnenberg, K.L., eds. Advancing the fundamental sciences. Proceedings, Forest Service national earth sciences conference. Gen. Tech. Rep. PNW-689. Portland, OR: U.S. Department of Agriculture, Forest Service, Pacific Northwest Research Station: 118–130.

Liston, G.E.; Elder, K. 2006a. A meteorological distribution system for high-resolution terrestrial modeling (MicroMet). Journal of Hydrometeorology. 7(2): 217–234.

Liston, G.E.; Elder, K. 2006b. A distributed snow-evolution modeling system (SnowModel). Journal of Hydrometeorology. 7(6): 1259–1276.

Liston, G.E.; Hiemstra, C. 2008. A simple data assimilation system for complex snow distributions (SnowAssim). Journal of Hydrometeorology. 9(5): 989–1004.

Lugo, A.E.; Swanson, F.J.; Gonzalez, O.R., et al. 2006. Long-term research at the USDA Forest Service's experimental forests and ranges. BioScience. 56(1): 39–48.

Montesi, J.; Elder, K.; Schmidt, R.A.; Davis, R.E. 2004. Sublimation of intercepted snow within a subalpine forest canopy at two elevations. Journal of Hydrometeorology. 5: 763–773.

National Research Council (NRC). 2008. Hydrologic effects of a changing forest landscape. Washington, DC: National Academy of Sciences. 180 p.

Negron, J.F.; Popp, J.B. 2004. Probability of ponderosa pine infestation by mountain pine beetle in the Colorado Front Range. Forest Ecology and Management. 191(1–3): 17–27.

Orme, A.R.; Bailey, R.G. 1970. The effect of vegetation conversion and flood discharge on stream channel geometry: the case of southern California watersheds. Proceedings, Association of American Geographers meeting. Washington, DC: Association of American Geographers. 12: 101–106.

Reid, L.M.; Lewis, J. 2007. Rates and implications of rainfall interception in a coastal redwood forest. In: Standiford, R.B.; Giusti, G.A.; Valachovic, Y., et al., eds. What does the future hold? Proceedings, redwood region forest science symposium. Gen. Tech. Rep. PSW-GTR-194. Albany, CA: U.S. Department of Agriculture, Forest Service, Pacific Southwest Research Station: 107–117.

Rutter, N.; Essery, R.; Pomeroy, J., et al. 2009. Evaluation of forest snow processes models (SnowMIP2). Journal of Geophysical Research. 114; D06111, doi:10.1029/2008JD011063.

Schaberg, P.G.; DeHayes, D.H.; Hawley, G.J., et al. 2000. Acid mist and soil Ca and Al alter the mineral nutrition and physiology of red spruce. Tree Physiology. 20(2): 78–85.

Stednick, J. 1996. Monitoring the effects of timber harvest on annual water yield. Journal of Hydrology. 176: 79–95.

Stednick, J.; Ice, G.; Hale, V. 2006. Persistence and detectability of hydrologic changes following multiple timber harvest entries in the Oregon Coast Range: Alsea revisited. Eos Transactions. American Geophysical Union. 87(52): Fall Meet. Suppl., Abstract B21F-04.

Swank, W.T.; Vose, J.M.; Elliott, K.J. 2001. Long-term hydrologic and water quality responses following commercial clearcutting of mixed hardwoods on a southern Appalachian catchment. Forest Ecology and Management. 143: 163–178.

Troendle, C.A.; King, R.M. 1985. The effect of timber harvest on the Fool Creek watershed, 30 years later. Water Resources Research. 21(12): 1915–1922.

Troendle, C.A.; Leaf, C.F. 1980. Hydrology. In: An approach to water resources evaluation of non-point silvicultural sources. EPA-600/8-80-012. Athens, GA: U.S. Environmental Protection Agency: 1–173. Chapter III.

Westerling, A.L.; Hidalgo, H.G.; Cayan, P.R.; Swetnam, T.W. 2006. Warming and earlier spring increase Western U.S. forest wildfire activity. Science. 313: 940–943.

Lessons Learned From Synthesizing the North American Long-Term Soil Productivity Study and Cool Results

D. Andrew Scott[1]

Abstract

In the mid-1980s, concerns regarding the sustainable productivity of our Nation's public and private forests abounded as a result of a number of scientific reports from the 1960s through 1980s that questioned the sustainability of forest productivity under managed systems. As a result of the National Forest Management Act of 1976, the national forests needed clear guidance on the sustainability of managed forests and turned to Forest Service Research and Development for help. Discussions were held in 1986 that culminated in a national plan, approved in 1989, that established a cooperative study between Forest Service Research and the National Forest System to address these questions. This unique partnership, called the North American Long-Term Soil Productivity Study, is the longest running coordinated research program in the Forest Service. The first installation was established in 1990 on the Palustris Experimental Forest near Alexandria, LA. Since then, more than 60 core installations and another 40 affiliate installations have been established across the United States and Canada, cutting across many agency and private sectors and making this study the largest of its kind in the world.

The study elegantly and carefully examines the impacts of organic matter removal (bole-only harvest, whole-tree harvest, and complete site organic matter harvest) and soil compaction (none, moderate, severe) on tree growth and development, soil density, soil fertility, and biological functioning, and the development of the understory ecology. Fifteen years of findings have shown that initial concerns with soil compaction were largely unfounded, because few sites show any negative impacts from soil compaction. Some sites show increased tree growth due to improved water holding capacity or to control of understory vegetation. Conversely, several sites have begun to exhibit losses of productivity as a result of removing more organic matter than just the merchantable bole, which raises questions about intensive harvesting for biofuels on both public and private lands. Continued work is under way to elucidate the various mechanisms associated with these results on the various sites and to develop practical guidelines for national forest managers.

Several major lessons have been learned from this cooperative effort. One lesson is that sustained success depends on a theme that has universal relevancy (sustained productivity). Another is that the experimental thrust must stay on track but also must be flexible enough to address other important themes that emerge over time (e.g., susceptibility/resistance to wildfire, carbon sequestration). We found that success requires vision, tenacity, and creativity of a core cadre of committed individuals—all of whom had personal influence on the design and conduct of the effort. A final lesson is that success can continue only if scientists and managers freely share relevant information. Now in its 19th year of existence, this grassroots research network is poised to deliver the long-term data needed to sustainably manage the timber lands of North America.

[1] Research Soil Scientist, U S Department of Agriculture Forest Service, Southern Research Station, Pineville, LA

Modeling Mortality on Long-Term Growth Plots in Kentucky, New York, Ohio, and Pennsylvania With Consideration of the Effects of Future Climate Change

Daniel A. Yaussy[1] and Louis R. Iverson[2]

Abstract

Individual tree measurements have been collected periodically on sites established in Kentucky, New York, Ohio, and Pennsylvania to investigate the effects of thinning on the growth and yield of valuable hardwood tree species. These plots were installed as long ago as 1959 and as recently as 1985. The long-term characteristics of this data set allow the investigation of climate effects on the mortality of individual trees. Monthly and annual regional temperature, precipitation, and Palmer Drought Severity Index were associated with mortality through Cox Regression Survival Analysis. The model produced with the survival analysis was then run using future climate predictions from conservative and extremely general circulation models to estimate possible future mortality rates.

[1] Research Forester, U S Department of Agriculture (USDA) Forest Service, Northern Research Station, Delaware, OH

[2] Ecologist, USDA Forest Service, Northern Research Station, Delaware, OH

Using Long-Term Regeneration Data From Multiple Studies To Extend and Operationalize Ecological Theory

David L. Loftis[1] and Tara L. Keyser[1]

Abstract

The portfolio of research associated with a designated forest research field facility typically consists of both case studies and studies with replicated field designs. This observation is particularly true on research sites whose establishment predates the widespread use of experimental statistics, but case studies with pretreatment data collection and posttreatment evaluation of outcomes have continued to be installed for a variety of reasons. Both kinds of studies can be valuable sources of inference.

In this paper, we synthesize the data from a relatively large number of studies of natural regeneration treatments applied to southern Appalachian hardwood stands. The stands were located on the Bent Creek Experimental Forest or in national forests nearby. The focus of the synthesis is the development of a working hypothesis consistent with some contemporary concepts of succession that provides the basis for a model to predict species composition following regeneration harvests. A modeling framework is suggested, along with one approach to validating and updating the model.

[1] Research Forester, U S Department of Agriculture Forest Service, Southern Research Station, Asheville, NC

Meeting Current and Future Conservation Challenges Through the Synthesis of Long-Term Silviculture and Range Management Research

55

Quantitative Syntheses for Operational-Scale Thinning Studies in Douglas-Fir

Duncan S. Wilson[1] and Paul D. Anderson[2]

Large-scale management experiments (LSMEs) in young forests are a critical part of adaptive management of natural resources on public lands. Several such operational studies were initiated in young Douglas-fir forests in the Pacific Northwest Research Station (PNW) to test approaches for restoration thinning and for enhancing late-seral habitat for several plant and animal species. Various density management treatments were implemented to reduce overstory tree density, promote spatial heterogeneity at several scales (McComb et al. 1993), and increase understory vegetation growth and diversity. Treatments were designed to redirect forest development to emulate that following natural disturbance and to possibly accelerate development of late-seral forest structures (Tappeiner et al. 1997). Treatment units are relatively large (20 to 60 ha) and were explicitly designed to encompass multiple home ranges of many songbirds and small mammals. The large treatment units enable testing for population changes following the thinning treatments.

Passive-adaptive management relies on understanding and creating stand and landscape forest structures that are similar to natural, unmanaged systems and are therefore assumed to provide sufficient habitat for conserving biodiversity (Spies 1991). This approach is similar to the coarse filter approach to biological conservation (Hunter 1990). This critical assumption underpinning passive management normally remains untested, greatly increasing conservation risk especially in PNW forests where structural legacies from past management have profoundly altered forest development (Tappeiner et al. 1997). In addition, passive management provides little guidance on how conservation risk may increase due to timber production or on how to manage for special habitat needs of sensitive species. In contrast, active-adaptive management relies on broad-scale

testing of new management ideas under operational conditions. Examples of active-adaptive management have been over entire fisheries or similarly extensive areas (Walters 1986). LSMEs are designed, manipulative studies of management options, and, despite the large experimental installations, these studies cover a minute portion of the forested land base under management, and they carry low risk from failing to meet management objectives. Thus, they fall intermediate between the passive and active approach to adaptive management (Walters 1986).

Despite the advantages of designed, manipulative experiments, each study has relatively low replication and low statistical power to test for treatment differences. The layout, treatment, and management costs in these studies are prohibitively high, which limits replication (Monserud 2002). Moreover, replications are usually geographically and often floristically distinct. Little to no attempt was made to reduce variability within—or between—blocks (Monserud 2002) and in this respect, the study designs have many similarities to replicated case studies (Yin 2003). Even when studies are in the same broad forest type (e.g., young Douglas-fir forests in Oregon), data collection and the suite of wildlife studies are often different between studies (Poage and Anderson 2007), so synthesis of research findings across studies is rare. These challenges with operational experiments are not unique to forest management; however, managers rely on study findings, and developing effective approaches to research synthesis remains a priority.

The primary objective of this study was to test the suitability of meta-analysis for synthesizing research findings across studies in these forested systems. This study is focused on the meta-analysis aspect of research synthesis; however, management insights come from a number of synthesis approaches. Specifically, results from a parallel hierarchical Bayesian analysis are presented for better insight into the specific questions addressed in the meta-analysis. The approach is consistent with the original intent of the LSMEs. Often, meta-analyses in natural

[1] Assistant Professor, Oklahoma State University, Stillwater, OK

[2] Supervisory Research Forester, U S Department of Agriculture Forest Service, Pacific Northwest Research Station, Corvallis, OR

resource management will focus on general hypotheses in an attempt to generalize across different regions or even continents (Rosenvald and Lohmus 2008). These broad-scale questions often do not address the very specific questions faced by managers (e.g., will thinning increase the risk of local extinction of a certain species?). To address focused, region-specific questions, the suitability of meta-analysis as a complement to more formal ecological modeling approaches, specifically hierarchical Bayesian models (Clark and Gelfand 2006), was evaluated.

Results from a parallel study on songbird responses to thinning (Wilson et al., in press) were used to guide hypothesis testing using meta-analysis. The songbird study used a hierarchical Bayesian approach to connect songbird surveys from three separate thinning studies in young Douglas-fir forests. The aim of that parallel study was to examine how differences in understory and overstory vegetation composition and structure modifies songbird responses to thinning and to possibly help explain inconsistent results across each study. Wilson et al. (in press) found that understory shrub cover and plant species richness strongly modified songbird response to thinning treatments for several species. Thinning units showed considerable variability in understory vegetation structure, and these differences altered the songbird community. In this current study, the general applicability of thinning for songbird conservation was examined. Specifically, the consistency of shrub cover and species richness responses to thinning across a larger set of studies and the similarity in response variability across studies were tested.

The meta-analysis in this current study focuses on parameter estimation and identifying response surfaces (Osenberg et al. 1999) rather than on the more usual hypothesis testing across representative studies. We used data from five LSMEs in western Oregon to test the magnitude and consistency of shrub response, species richness, and other vegetation components found to be important mediators of songbird response to thinning. The meta-analysis involved 80 experimental units, including unthinned controls and different severity thinning treatments. Specifically, we related understory vegetation response to thinning severity and tested the consistency of response across thinning units in order to address wildlife conservation goals.

Literature Cited

Clark, J.S.; Gelfand, A.E. 2006. A future for models and data in environmental science. Trends in Ecology & Evolution. 21: 375–380.

Hunter, M.L., Jr. 1990. Wildlife, forests, and forestry: principles of managing forests for biological diversity. Englewood Cliffs, NJ: Prentice Hall. 370 p.

McComb, W.C.; Spies, T.A.; Emmingham, W.H. 1993. Douglas-fir forests: managing for timber and mature-forest habitat. Journal of Forestry. 91: 31–42.

Monserud, R.A. 2002. Large-scale management experiments in the moist maritime forests of the Pacific Northwest. Landscape and Urban Planning. 59: 159–180.

Osenberg, C.W.; Sarnelle, O.; Cooper, S.D.; Holt, R.D. 1999. Resolving ecological questions through meta-analysis: goals, metrics, and models. Ecology. 80: 1105–1117.

Poage, N.J.; Anderson, P.D. 2007. Large-scale management experiments of western Oregon and Washington: a comprehensive and current overview. PNW-GTR-713. Portland, OR: U.S. Department of Agriculture, Forest Service, Pacific Northwest Research Station. 44 p.

Rosenvald, R.; Lohmus, A. 2008. For what, when and where is green-tree retention better than clear-cutting? A review of the biodiversity aspects. Forest Ecology and Management. 255: 1–15.

Spies, T.A. 1991. Plant species diversity and occurrences in young, mature and old-growth Douglas-fir stands in western Oregon and Washington. Gen. Tech. Rep. PNW-GTR-285. Portland, OR: U.S. Department of Agriculture, Forest Service, Pacific Northwest Research Station: 111–121.

Tappeiner, J.C.; Huffman, D.; Marshall, D., et al. 1997. Density, ages, and growth rates in old-growth and young-growth forests in coastal Oregon. Canadian Journal of Forest Research. 27: 638–648.

Walters, C.J. 1986. Adaptive management of renewable resources. New York: Macmillan. 374 p.

Wilson, D.S.; Anderson, P.D.; Puettmann, K.J. [In press]. Evaluating the consistency of understory vegetation response to forest thinning through synthesis. Forestry.

Yin, R.K. 2003. Case study research: design and methods. Thousand Oaks, CA: Sage Publications. 180 p.

On Conducting a Multisite, Multidisciplinary Forestry Research Project: Lessons From the National Fire and Fire Surrogate Study

James D. McIver[1] and C. Phillip Weatherspoon[2]

Abstract

The national Fire and Fire Surrogates (FFS) study is described, from its conceptual stage in early 1996 to the completion of its short-term phase in May 2006. Comprising 12 sites, the FFS is a comprehensive multidisciplinary experiment designed to evaluate the economics and ecological consequences of alternative fuel reduction treatments in seasonally dry forests of the United States. The FFS employs a common experimental design across the 12-site network, with each site consisting of a fully replicated experiment that compares four treatments: (1) an unmanipulated control, (2) prescribed fire, (3) mechanical treatments, and (4) mechanical plus prescribed fire treatments. We measured operational costs and variables within several components of the ecosystem, including vegetation, the fuel bed, soils, bark beetles, tree diseases, and wildlife in the same 10-ha experimental units. This design allowed us to assemble a fairly complete picture of ecosystem response to treatment at the site scale and to compare treatment response across a wide variety of conditions. We offer the FFS as a model for conducting a complex, multidisciplinary management experiment focused on natural resource issues. We then discuss why we believe it was successful and how it could be improved. We discuss seven key features that we believe must be considered to conduct a successful multidisciplinary experiment: (1) funding, (2) design, (3) partnerships, (4) organization, (5) standardization, (6) data management, and (7) outreach. Although experiments such as the FFS are difficult to execute, they may be our best hope for answering some of our more pressing questions in the field of natural resource management.

[1] Associate Professor, Oregon State University, Union, OR

[2] Research Forester (retired), U S Department of Agriculture Forest Service, Pacific Southwest Research Station, Redding, CA

Novel Statistical Techniques for Synthesizing Complex Data: Descriptions of Short Courses

The Use and Application of Meta-Analysis in Forest Science

Meta-analysis is a technique specifically designed for the statistical synthesis of data from independent experiments (Gurevitch and Hedges 1999). Meta-analysis expresses the results of each experiment in the form of an "effect size," which is expressed on a common scale across studies. This method helps overcome the problem of reduced statistical power in studies with small sample sizes by analyzing the results from a group of studies and allows for the comparison of independent experiments that have different metrics of response. Although largely developed within the medical community, meta-analysis is being increasingly used in a variety of environmental applications.

This course will offer a short introduction to the meta-analysis technique, present a range of applications for this method, and provide a hands-on computer lab to introduce participants to meta-analytic computer software. Standard data sets will be offered for instructional use. The instructor, Dr. Lindsey Rustad, is a research forest ecologist with the Northern Research Station (NRS07), located in Durham, NH. She previously conducted two major meta-analyses: one on the effects of ecosystem warming on soil respiration, nitrogen mineralization, and net primary productivity in terrestrial ecosystems and one on the effects of experimental nitrogen additions of forested ecosystems. She is currently conducting a meta-analysis on the response of terrestrial ecosystems to experimental changes in the magnitude and timing of precipitation.

Literature Cited

Gurevitch, J.; Hedges, L.V. 1999. Statistical issues in ecological meta-analyses. Ecology. 80(4): 1142–1149.

Structural Equation Modeling

Ecologists deal with research settings that are complex and multivariate in nature. Modern advances in statistical analysis, such as structural equation modeling (SEM), improve our ability to draw causal inference from multivariate data that are collected in both experimental and nonexperimental settings and improve our ability to test our theories on the structure and function of complex systems. In this seminar, I will provide a brief overview of the mathematical underpinnings of SEM, a conceptual visualization of SEM and what it can do, examples of SEM models that might be useful in ecological research, and examples of how to set up and implement each model type using a popular analysis program, LISREL. Participants will be provided with a CD that will include the seminar's PowerPoint presentation, example LISREL programs, and data sets to implement the examples discussed in the presentation.

This short course will be presented by Dr. Bruce Pugesek, a research statistician with the U.S. Geological Survey located at the Northern Rocky Mountain Science Center in Bozeman, MT. Dr. Pugesek has developed and applied SEM as a technique in long-term research on avian ecology. He is the editor and coauthor of a book titled *Structural Equation Modeling: Applications in Ecological and Evolutionary Biology.*

Hierarchical Modeling for Ecological Projects

Hierarchical models are rapidly transforming the way ecologists do inference. The good news is that techniques now available to anyone with a computer can be used to address complex inferential problems. Students in environmental sciences can become quite sophisticated over the course of a Ph.D. program that combines coursework and plenty of hands-on application.

The challenge is that one cannot master these topics in a single meeting. Moreover, the group will have a range of backgrounds. I will try to give you a sense of the potential and some concrete applications with data. We will try to get a "feel" for how hierarchical models are constructed (modeling), how they are analyzed (computation), and what they can do for us. We will use many examples coming from me and your own research to demonstrate how models are constructed and then analyzed using computational tools.

To get started, the basic building blocks for hierarchical models are likelihoods and priors. Hierarchical models organize these pieces into graphs having several levels. These are the knowns (data and priors) and the unknowns (latent processes and parameter values). Hierarchical models do not have to be Bayesian, but they usually are because it is very logical to think of inference this way:

$$p(unknowns|knowns) = p(process, parameters|data, priors)$$

This structure comes naturally to a Bayesian. It is unwieldy to the non-Bayesian. A hierarchical model typically breaks this down as:

$$p(process, parameters|data, priors) =$$
$$p(data|process, parameters)p(process|parameters)$$
$$p(parameters|priors)$$

It turns out that this structure is amenable to simulation, using Markov Chain Monte Carlo, specifically Gibbs, sampling.

For the short course, I hope to accomplish the following:

- Summarize the Bayesian paradigm—likelihood, prior, posterior, and prediction.
- Introduce basic concepts of hierarchical modeling—how to factor a complicated problem; some basic distributions.
- Introduce the idea behind Gibbs sampling—the concepts and some simple examples in R.
- Discuss more advanced applications.

I will provide examples, with explanation, code, and data sets adapted from the lab manual that is available from Princeton University Press.

Dr. Jim Clark is the Blomquist Professor of the Nicholas School of the Environment, professor of biology, and professor of statistics and decision science at Duke University. Dr. Clark's research focuses on how global change affects forests. His lab is using long-term experiments and monitoring studies to determine disturbance and climate controls on the dynamics of 20th-century forests in combination with extensive modeling to forecast ecosystem change. Included in his extensive publishing record are three books addressing ecological modeling methods: *Models for Ecological Data* (Princeton University Press, 2007), *Models for Ecological Data in R* (Princeton University Press, 2007), and *Hierarchical Models of the Environment* (Oxford University Press, 2006).

Part 2
Notes From the Breakout Sessions

Introduction

During the Forest Service Silviculture and Range Management Synthesis Workshop, concurrent breakout sessions were conducted for the purpose of identifying opportunities for synthesis and collaboration across experimental forests and ranges. Four breakout topics were (1) vegetation composition, structure, and productivity; (2) water and vegetation management; (3) biomass for energy; and (4) climate change.

Each breakout group discussed the management activities that should be implemented to address the breakout topic. All groups were provided a specific set of questions to address during the breakout session. These five questions were as follows:

1. What are the critical questions to be answered relative to the topic (synthesis topics)?

2. What data are in hand to address these questions (data inventory)?

3. How could an effort be structured to answer these questions with information in hand (outline pathway and realistic timeline) and who will work on these synthesis agreement(s)?

4. What products will be delivered from the group's discussions and timeline (expected products)?

5. What is needed for successful synthesis efforts that we don't have or don't think we have (list of needs, e.g., available digital data, easy-share data network, skills/facilities, money)?

The following report summarizes the results from these concurrent breakout sessions. The group leaders for each breakout group are identified for possible followup.

Breakout Session 1

Synthesis Group for Vegetation Composition, Structure, and Productivity

Dave Loftis[1] and Eric Knapp[2]

The vegetation composition, structure, and productivity group began with a general discussion concerning the state of experimental forests with respect to the call to identify critical questions facing experimental forests regarding vegetation composition and structure. The initial discussion was lively. Although the discussion was informational in illustrating a variety of issues being dealt with by experimental forests, the topics did not fully stay within the bounds of vegetation composition structure. The initial commentary was distilled into seven important questions to address the first question asked of the breakout groups.

Further discussion from the seven questions led moderators to ask, "What is the most important issue facing our experimental forests with respect to vegetative composition structure?" Individual observations by the group are reflected in the numbered responses.

On the second day, some controversy arose with regard to several issues. This controversy is worth noting because it points to potential discord between competing issues surrounding experimental forest use, research, and stewardship. Questions raised in the numbered responses in the following text also illustrate the broad variety of opinion among participants on the role and competing interests of both scientists and management on experimental forests. Moderators asked a followup question based on these discussions: Whether all competing (research) interests within the experimental forests could be met under the umbrella of a single philosophy or goal statement.

Session moderators focused the discussion on developing a synthesis statement, a set of goals, and appropriate action items for the session during the final hour. Session participants thought the resulting synthesis statement (see question 4) was adequate, as were the action items, although participants agreed that these items were just a foundation of what should come in the near future through followup efforts.

Question 1. What are the critical questions to be answered relative to the topic (synthesis topics)?

- How does disturbance type/intensity change forests?
  - Do we have enough data for the following (gradient of low/medium/high)?
    - Characterization of disturbance type/intensity.
    - Response to disturbance type/intensity.
    - Do we have sufficient temporal scale and spatial scale?
- How can we adapt forests through management to climate change?
- Can forest communities shift fast enough relative to climate change?
- What stand structures/composition would be most resilient to climate change and associated disturbance? How many of us (at the conference) have old-growth-associated data/ information for baseline comparison? Yes = 22 out of 29 EFs present (see table 1).
- How many have metadata for meteorological data of at least 10 years? Yes = 18/29.
- How have stands/communities changed over time?
- How does variation in stand structure over time influence productivity?
- How do we scale from stand-level structures to landscape patterns necessary to address responses associated with larger spatial scales?

---

[1] Research Forester, U S Department of Agriculture (USDA) Forest Serice, Southern Research Station, Asheville, NC

[2] Research Ecologist, USDA Forest Service, Pacific Southwest Research Station, Redding, CA

Question 2. What data are in hand to address these questions (data inventory)?

In order to discuss what data were available, the group identified a subset of metadata categories into which the majority of work being completed would fall. By creating this metadata table (table 1), a further discussion of what data were available would then be possible.

As table 1 indicates, a large amount of current (and historical) vegetative data are available to researchers. One key question raised concerning this data was its compilation into a comprehensive database.

The concern that data were not being entered into databases for use after their acquisition was raised for both current and historical studies. The group conceded that many regional offices contained "treasure troves" of unused "raw" vegetative study data.

Table 1.—*In-room tally of experimental forest study activity.[a] This table will be developed further as a byproduct of this workshop and expanded to include all 80 Experimental Forests and Ranges (EFRs) and a link to specific EFRs.*

Studies include?	Yes	No
Clear-cuts:	24	5
Shelterwood:	21	8
Seedtree:	7	22
Single tree selection:	21	8
2 age structures:	15	14
Group selection	12	17
Control:	22	7
Thinning studies:	25	4
Fire studies:	18	11
Herbicide apps:	10	19
Grazing studies:	5	24
Herbicide apps:	7	22
Fertilization:	9	20
Non-woody veg:	24	5
Natural disturbance:	12	17
Insects:	9	20
Disease:	15	14
Invasive plants:	15	14
Invasive insects:	2	27
Exotic diseases:	6	23

[a] N = 29 experimental forests represented by breakout session attendees.

Problems were perceived regarding the state of the data. Not all data collected were in usable formats (presumably). Therefore, the group suggested and discussed methods of cataloguing what data were available and how to organize them into a consistent format. There was no clear consensus reached about format, due to the complexity and variety of data, but the point remained that a consistent data format should be attained when possible.

The scope of data and how to approach it directly was not successfully addressed; however, the idea of a metadata storehouse containing a list of available data for study was included in the action items proposed by the vegetative session. Development of this metadata storehouse would be the first step in organizing the data itself.

Question 3. How could an effort be structured to answer these questions with information in hand (outline pathway and realistic timeline) and who will work on this synthesis agreement(s)?

As previously mentioned, the group discussed the formation of a metadata database due to the lack of knowledge of what information is available to researchers. Goals included the following:

- Create a database template (6-month timeline).
- Populate the metadata database.
  - List current studies and those available in electronic format by the end of fiscal year 2009.
  - Include historical (closed) studies, and those not available in electronic format (those on paper only, for example).

Question 4. What products will be delivered from the group's discussions and timeline (expected products)?

Before the culmination of the breakout session, the moderators led the group to a solid consensus concerning important topics and action items surrounding vegetative composition on experimental forests. Nearly the entire group participated in a roundtable-like discussion that clarified the goals of the attendees. There was acknowledgment that more work was necessary, but the following discussions were a strong start to the process.

Synthesis: What have we learned from long-term silvicultural and ecological studies on experimental forests and other associated sites that can guide future management?

- Productivity.
- Regeneration.
- Composition/diversity/structure.
- Resistance/resilience to disturbance.

The group anticipated that its efforts would facilitate work done by other breakout session groups. Efforts would also assist with an update or revision of the *Silvicultural Systems Handbook*.

Question 5. What is needed for successful synthesis efforts that we don't have or don't think we have (list of needs); e.g., available digital data, easy-share data network, skills/facilities, money?

This question was not directly addressed by the group; however, during the course of the discussion, several needs were mentioned. An easily accessible central method of locating available data should be created and maintained. Another focus should be digitizing data that is not currently available in electronic format, such as historical data from years before the use of computers. One difficulty in digitizing data would be budget constraints—currently no budget is available to maintain or create such a database system and funds would have to be acquired in order to create and maintain it.

Breakout Session 2

Synthesis Group for Water and Vegetation Management

Mary Beth Adams[1] and Ward McCaughey[2]

Question 1. What are the critical questions to be answered relative to the topic (synthesis topics)?

The water and vegetation management group identified its interest in long-term studies and the effects of water and vegetation by discussing ways in which to incorporate and synthesize data pertaining to climate, vegetation distribution, disturbance history, and geology of the Experimental Forests and Ranges (EFRs) sites. Most experimental forest watersheds have a history of logging or other disturbances, and, with this information, the group discussed how the knowledge of these legacy effects could be used to illustrate watershed evolution. This approach would allow for an assessment of the current health and conditions of such systems, which could possibly aid in the development of future management practices among these watersheds. The water and vegetation management group identified four priority questions to address these issues:

1. What are the effects/linkages of vegetation management—and potential other disturbances—on/to hydrology? This is ongoing work, and will lead to a series of publications.

2. What are the legacies of earlier management and their impacts—and cumulative effects—on watersheds? What does this mean for new management practices?

3. What is the inherent variability of water quality (e.g., nutrients, sediment, sediment budgets, water temperature, air temperature, and dissolved organic carbon)?

4. Is climate change affecting water supply? Can we predict effects of changes in climate on water supply?

In addition, a number of "higher up in the tree" research issues were identified:

- Effects of riparian zone management and processes.

- Land use change and water dynamics (partnering with other agencies using EFRs as experimental references).

- Valuation of water as an ecosystem service.

- Linking biological to physical and chemical stream characteristics.

- Using climate data from EFRs to understand how spatial climate variability predisposes systems to the effects of vegetation change (amount and vitality, species composition).

Question 2. What data are in hand to address these questions (data inventory)?

This question was not directly addressed by the group; however, it was mentioned that there are quite a few experiments conducted on small, gauged watersheds of EFRs that collect similar data. For watersheds that are not gauged (e.g., larger watersheds), additional data inventory will be necessary. Hydrodb/Climdb is a Web harvester that searches available data from gauged watersheds. There is a significant amount of information available from gauged watersheds, but to bring it together for synthesis still requires considerable effort.

[1] Supervisory Soil Scientist, U S Department of Agriculture (USDA) Forest Service, Northern Research Station, Parsons, WV

[2] Research Forester, USDA Forest Service, Rocky Mountain Research Station, Missoula, MT

Question 3. How could an effort be structured to answer these with information in hand (outline pathway and realistic timeline) and who will work on this synthesis agreement(s)?

We did not directly address this question. See below.

Question 4. What products will be delivered from the group's discussions and timeline (expected products)?

The products of this group's research efforts would be to publish peer-reviewed journal articles addressing the following issues:

- The effects/linkages of vegetation management and other disturbances to hydrology.
- The variability of water quality across EFRs.
- The impact of climate change on water supply.

A targeted workshop will be held in the spring of 2010 in conjunction with National Council for Air and Stream Improvement on nutrient variability in streams to help States understand the issue of variability relative to nutrient criteria (for standard setting). In addition, posters, outreach fliers, nonscientific popular press articles, and targeted workshops pertaining to these issues will be implemented.

Question 5. What is needed for successful synthesis efforts that we don't have or don't think we have (list of needs); e.g., available digital data, easy-share data network, skills/facilities, money?

The water and vegetation management group identified a "Directory of Context for Experimental Watersheds" as a pressing research need for synthesis. In order to put the metadata of our nationwide watersheds into context—and document what data are available—the group proposed the creation of a position funded by the Washington Office. By creating this funded position, a database could then be created at all EFRs with watershed data and eventually for all EFRs. The outcome of this funded position would be a database created for all participating EFRs, with the potential to be used for meta-analysis studies.

Breakout Session 3

Synthesis Group for Biomass for Energy

Marilyn Buford[1] and Joseph McNeel[2]

Question 1. What are the critical questions to be answered relative to the topic (synthesis topics)?

The biomass for energy synthesis group identified four priority questions to address during their discussion:

1. What is the availability now and into the future of wood for energy? (Where availability equals affordability, accessibility, infrastructure, conversion processes, and is a function of time, bio-geo-physical [weather] factors, policy, and technology.)

2. What are sustainable management inputs, prescriptions, and regimes that optimize (cost effectiveness and resource use efficiency) the production and supply (cost and yield) of wood energy?

3. What are the factors that can affect the use of wood-based fossil fuel substitutes (sensitivity analysis)?

4. How much can be sustainably removed? (Sustainable equals soil quality and productivity, water quality and quantity, and services and functions.)

Question 2. What data are in hand to address these questions (data inventory)?

To address the availability and future of wood for energy, the biomass for energy group considered the following data: the *Billion Ton Report* (BTR) plus related analyses; BTR update; regional- and State-based studies; byproduct inventories; forest inventory and analysis data; Timber Products Output data; road/bridge and transportation/distribution databases

(U.S. Department of Transportation, States, counties); logger/equipment availability; and current and potential technology. Data considered for identifying sustainable management inputs and prescriptions and regimes that optimize the production and supply of wood energy included the following: nutrient studies, competition control, vegetation management and silvicultural studies, genetics, species selection, density studies, whole-tree logging studies, Long-Term Soil Productivity (LTSP) Study, life cycle analysis, short rotation woody crops, precommercial thinning and thinning studies, machine and system interaction studies (logging), salvage and residual/removal studies, harvest intensity studies, and biomass allometric studies. It was decided among the group that question two could be addressed immediately with the given data in hand if database product design was considered. The product is "Management systems for optimizing the supply of energy wood from our Nation's forests: Solutions from long-term silvicultural and forest management studies (regionalized)."

In order to address the factors that can affect the use of wood-based fossil fuel substitutes, the group concluded that no data were readily available and that current and existing databases offered little or no sensitivity related information. Finally, to address the priority question regarding how much can be sustainably removed, the group considered this available data: LTSP, watershed management studies, site-specific habitat/wildlife responses, whole-tree harvesting studies, carbon and nitrogen status, nutrient drain/slash conservation studies, site preparation studies, terrain and soil operability studies, digital elevation models, land cover inventories, soil databases, acid deposition studies, harvest intensity studies, and biomass allometric studies.

[1] National Silviculture Program Leader, U S Department of Agriculture Forest Service, Washington, DC

[2] Director, West Virginia University, Division of Forestry and Natural Resources, Morgantown, WV

Question 3. How could an effort be structured to answer these with information in hand (outline pathway and realistic timeline) and who will work on this synthesis agreement(s)?

- Organize key references, studies, and databases by matrix (see table 2).
- Create a set of usable databases (descriptive, accessible data) for online delivery.
- Link data from studies with stand dynamics models to produce size class distributions (biomass allocation distribution).
- Conduct sensitivity analysis of linked models.
- Create a user-friendly, Web-based "what if" modeling system (not just Web dashboard delivery), as well as traditional delivery systems (extension, workshop).
- Identify critical knowledge gaps and target research/repurpose existing studies.

Table 2.—*Theorized data matrix format.*

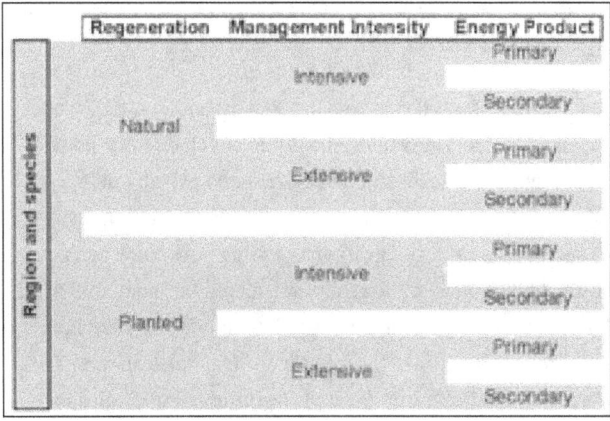

Question 4. What products will be delivered from the group's discussions and timeline (expected products)?

- Catalog and archive data into a database that is accessible on line for public use. This catalog would be obtained by classifying the data into a matrix of different classification themes. For example, a matrix of the following form could provide insights into categories of data that can be collected and structured:

    MATRIX example = (Region [1 ,2, 3…] X Regeneration {natural, plantation} X Silvicultural system [1, 2,. n] X Energy products [primary, secondary])

- Develop site-level information on the productivity of biomass; i.e., information on managing the forest resources to obtain the optimal products in different regions for natural as well as plantation systems.
- Design expert systems that can help decide how to produce biomass resources as primary products in different regions by identifying/assigning appropriate prescriptions, resources, management options, etc. This system should also be Web based and available for public use.

Question 5. What is needed for successful synthesis efforts that we don't have or don't think we have (list of needs); e.g., available digital data, easy-share data network, skills/facilities, money?

The biomass for energy group identified the following skills as necessary for following its proposed pathways for designing a matrix and expert systems:

- Leadership visioning/project management (core team consisting of three to four people and a regional representative).
- Detective/critical thinking/critical knowledge (filters).
- Systems modeling/silviculture-biometrics/programming skills.
- Object-oriented programming/client-server architecture/database management/Web programming/user needs/access/user-friendly interface skills.

The following resources were proposed and must be available in order to achieve the desired products:

- Money, team of people, and a leader.
- Model and Web program developer.
- Digitizer (data entry, qualitative/quantitative).

Breakout Session 4

Synthesis Group for Climate Change

Paul Anderson[1] and Martin Vavra[2]

Question 1. What are the critical questions to be answered relative to the topic (synthesis topics)?

The climate change group began its discussion by separating the effects of climate change on vegetation into three main categories: (1) the physical environment, (2) the biological component, and (3) disturbance in terms of the extremes in both the physical environment and vegetation responses. Based on this framework, the group made a motion to come up with five priority questions that would address climate change using the breakdown of the physical environment, biological, and disturbance effects. The critical priority questions proposed by the climate change breakout session group included the following:

1. Do the EFRs' historical meteorological, hydrological, and other physical databases provide signals consistent with the hypothesis of climate change?

2. Are the EFRs' site-level historical meteorological, hydrological, and other physical data consistent with other regional climate/hydrological networks or models?

3. Given validation of the physical data, can biological data be evaluated to detect biological responses to the dynamics of the physical data?

   • Are there changes in forest composition, including exotics, which could be associated with a climate change signal?

4. How will climate change effects be distributed at various scales?

   • Among ecosystem components (life forms, taxa), including species or genotypes.

   • Across the landscape at various spatial scales (patterns).

   • Temporally (diurnal, seasonal, annular variation).

5. How should we manage under climate uncertainty?

   • What are robust systems for ecological classification given climate uncertainty?

   • What management approaches can be used to decrease risks or vulnerabilities to a changing climate?

   • What manipulative experiments should be conducted on EFRs to develop management approaches for adaptation and mitigation of climate change?

   • What are the sociopolitical considerations, including the National Environmental Policy Act, for doing climate change experiments on EFRs?

   • At what scales should management for uncertainty (risk management) be considered?

Question 2. What data are in hand to address these questions (data inventory)?

The next topic discussed focused on data needed to address these priority questions. The group identified the need to integrate meteorological and watershed data already available from the EFRs as well as data gathered from specific EFRs that measure water runoff and various soil characteristics to determine if a signal consistent with the hypothesis of climate change exists. The consensus of the group was that meteorological data would be most readily available, with hydrological data being available only on a subset of EFRs, and data such as soils and other physical characteristics would be least available. To address the vegetation component, the group decided that long-term vegetation studies from the EFRs, particularly studies with untreated controls or exclosures, would be ideal. An additional avenue for long-term vegetation data was through the use of dendrochronological studies, especially in areas with historical long-term vegetation data unavailable.

The source of data was then discussed by the climate change group. The group agreed on using regional EFR synthesis data

[1] Supervisory Research Forester, U S Department of Agriculture (USDA) Forest Service, Pacific Northwest Research Station, Corvallis, OR

[2] Supervisory Rangeland Scientist, USDA Forest Service, Pacific Northwest Research Station, La Grande, OR

in comparison to other outside sources (see priority question 2). Pathways were then discussed by the group, with the first pathway identified as the development of an inventory of data from EFRs. An inventory of all the available data from the EFRs would allow for an assessment of the data available for analyses as well as provide information on the potential of addressing these priority questions of climate change using EFR sites.

Question 3. How could an effort be structured to answer these with information in hand (outline pathway and realistic timeline) and who will work on this synthesis agreements(s)?

This topic was not discussed by the group. All EFRs with available data should be willing to participate in these efforts.

Question 4. What products will be delivered from the group's discussions and timeline (expected products)?

The products of this approach to addressing climate change by the EFRs would generate an assessment and matrix of the inventory data specifically related to climate change, the analysis results that would accompany these studies, and a manuscript of the results and findings.

Question 5. What is needed for successful synthesis efforts that we don't have or don't think we have (list of needs); e.g., available digital data, easy-share data network, skills/ facilities, money?

In order to complete the assessments and inventory, the defined needs of the group included dedicated staff time designated by the Washington Office to bring all these EFRs' synthesis data together. This staff time should be located in the field and plugged into the EFRs involved with syntheses efforts. The final need identified by the group was a meeting similar to this one, scheduled after the inventory data had been collected, in order to inform all parties interested of what particular data are available to address these climate change concerns.

Closing Session

The last day of the conference was reserved for each group to present its information and findings from the breakout session discussions and for participants to make final comments during a "potpourri session." The potpourri session was a forum in which all attendees could make very brief final comments about the conference and add any final input regarding material covered during the breakout or concurrent sessions during the week. The following text describes the comments and responses made during or after each breakout session group's presentation.

Comments From Breakout Session Reports

Comments made following the biomass for energy breakout session group presentation focused on using growth-and-yield models more effectively and the use of these models as a potential delivery system for work that has already been conducted on EFRs.

The second presentation was given by the vegetation composition, structure, and productivity breakout session group. Comments following this presentation emphasized the creation of a database matrix that could be used for all experimental forests. Additional feedback mentioned that a list of EFRs, starting with those that have productivity data (collected from 1970 to the present), should be listed in order of importance so that the information that the EFRs already have could be identified. The group presenters stressed the importance of the creation of a database matrix with some sort of descriptive filing structure that would allow for the examination of data on a particular forest type, region, stand level, etc. The final comment to this group was that in order for this database creation to occur and be accessible across all EFRs, some "supervisorial" intervention would likely need to occur.

The third presentation was made by the climate change breakout session group. The first comment to the presenters was that after the inventory assessment was completed, it would then be appropriate to reconvene so that others could see what syntheses could be done using the specific data that are available. The presenters responded that the success of the synthesis ties back to the assessment that is going to be done and that it will require resources to move this process forward. Another attendee questioned what would be done if the signals are not there to indicate climate change or if the signals do not match or correlate. The presenters commented that this hypothesis is the current one behind climate change and that the information collected on EFRs will be useful in deriving how these physical processes are being expressed in terms of their variation. The presenters also added that there is interesting information coming out about vegetation dynamics and that this recent information does not decrease the value of what is being done on EFRs. They stated that, across EFRs, there are plenty of opportunities to formulate syntheses around vegetation dynamics, which brings us back to our goal of addressing climate change.

The final breakout session presentation was given by the water and vegetation management group. One comment was made in regard to all presentations given. One individual stated that it would be appropriate, given the amount of synthesis that is going on, that we think long-term—maybe 3 years out—and organize a conference to enable representatives from all the EFRs to come together. This conference would be an opportunity to have scientists give presentations of their findings and processes they have been working on in terms of individual studies, synthesis work, and analyses. It was also added that this conference would provide an opportunity to invite constituents who would include not only the forest managers of the EFRs but other agencies outside the Forest Service, allowing for an extended network to be created in regard to syntheses efforts. It was suggested that a common database design might help move the momentum forward.

Conclusions and Recommendations From Breakout Sessions

Synthesis activities across EFRs would be greatly enhanced by better information about the research being done on EFRs and a description of data available.

Support is needed to develop tools for syntheses (metadata-bases) and for improving data availability.

Strong leadership is needed to help us manage our EFR resources as a network and to encourage and engage researchers from the Forest Service and our cooperators in synthesis activities.

We have a great opportunity in our network of EFRs and *must* keep the momentum going. There are too many important questions and research needs, including those discussed at this workshop, to not keep moving forward.

Appendix

Evaluating Long-Term Studies: Developing Criteria

Notes From a Voluntary Evening Session at the Workshop
September 30, 2008
Number of attendees: many; attendance not taken

The purpose of this session was to stimulate and initiate a discussion about a common framework for making resource allocations to long-term studies. The attendees acknowledge that there are special values associated with studies that have been carried out for a long time and that these values are not uniform across all such studies. We also acknowledge that, over time, the burden of sustaining measurements and treatments in existing long-term studies can pose a challenge for initiating new research. A consensus voluntary framework for allocating resources to long-term studies will help agency leaders and Experimental Forests and Ranges (EFRs) personnel make resource allocation decisions. Paul Anderson and Nathan Poage had already been working on developing such a framework.

We agreed that at some point we should also outline some strategies for the "rational mothballing" of studies to which resources are not currently being allocated so that it would be easy to find both the physical study sites and the associated data if their relevance increased in the future.

We took an informal poll of participants to produce a definition (in terms of a minimum length in years) of long-term research.

Minimum length (in years) of a "long-term study"	10	25	50
Number of participants who voted for this length	15	6	—

Discussants agreed that there is an implied hierarchy of research study values, from the local values to the scientists and stakeholders in individual EFRs through regional and national/agency values.

Many of the values can also be interpreted at these various levels. For example, the *strategic importance (importance to achieving agency, station, or Research Work Unit Description strategic goals)* of a study might be different at each of those levels. It is possible to imagine a study that is strategically important at a national or regional level, through its representation in a network that might not be important at the local level and vice versa.

That said, we listed several criteria of evaluation without specifying the level at which they are most important or how they might be interpreted at different levels of resource allocation:

- Rigor.
- Design.
- Data management.
- Prior relevance (historical value).
- Vision for future utility and relevance.
- Core variables.
- Cost/benefit of discoveries in real dollars.
- Scope of inference.
- Relation to strategic goals.
- Products anticipated.
- Superimposed research.
- Connection to/value of partner facilities and databases.
- Likelihood of maintaining custody.
- Security.
- Potential for manipulative research.
- Continuity of measurement and treatments.

We also recognized that, although we are discussing a study-level decision framework, we see a need for a strategic vision at the 80-forest level, and we identified some factors relevant to the development of a strategic vision at that level. These factors included the following (note that some are repeats from the previous list, and we could probably include most of the criteria in the previous list):

- Potential science questions for the future.

  • Desired future distribution of EFRs.

  • Potential decommissioning.

- Connections to and value of partner facilities and databases.

- Likelihood of maintaining custody and security.

- Potential of adding value with modest investment.

- Potential for manipulative research.

Finally, we agreed that our efforts, which we hope to continue through conference calls to develop an as-yet ill-defined product (possibly a publication or Web site) were complementary to the Washington Office effort to develop a business plan for EFRs, which is defined as a plan for managing assets and investments based on a combined bottom-up/top-down approach.

Susan Stout, Note Taker